The
Unwise
Monkey

Françoise Fautrel

ibooks

Habent Sua Fata Libelli

i

ibooks
Manhanset House
Shelter Island Hts., New York 11965-0342
Tel: 212-427-7139
bricktower@aol.com • www.ibooksinc.com
All rights reserved under the International and
Pan-American Copyright Conventions.
Printed in the United States by J. Boylston & Company, Publishers, New York.
No part of this publication may be reproduced, stored in a retrieval system, or
transmitted in any form or by any means, electronic, or otherwise, without the prior
written permission of the copyright holder. The ibooks colophon is a trademark of
J. Boylston & Company, Publishers.

Library of Congress Cataloging-in-Publication Data
Fautrel, Françoise
The Unwise Monkey
p. cm.
      1. Biography—Northern France 2. Biography—World War II
Non-fiction, I. Title.
  ISBN-13: 978-1-59687-994-2, Trade Paper

Copyright © 2015 Françoise Fautrel

May 2015

The Unwise Monkey

Françoise Fautrel

Acknowledgements:

I am grateful to Claire Baker for her encouragement and to both Maggie Kirtley and Maria Petrides for their patient and invaluable editorial help with this book.

CONTENTS

PART ONE

THE HELVETIC NIGHTMARE

Chapter One

The disappointment was immediate and total. I had expected to meet with my aunt Anna, a virtuous copy of my beautiful, but wayward mother. But the plain, frumpish woman, I met in the underpass of Lausanne's railway station was a terrible let down. Not even the tears she was shedding succeeded in moving me. The shock was too great. I was thirteen years old, and this age is without pity. I had come such a long way, waited so long for this meeting. I had survived for years, by hanging on to the hope, that one day Switzerland would welcome me in the open arms of a resurrected, beautiful, virtuous mother.

We sat facing each other on the train taking us from Lausanne to La Sarraz. My aunt had recovered her composure. She was explaining that having recently remarried, she had moved into her new husband's home. There was no room in the house, in which I could sleep. I would have to share the bedroom of the neighbours' baby in the flat below. I got an instant feeling not so much of "déja vu" but more of "déja experienced". Yes, I had not even set foot in the house that I was already farmed out. I was feeling very tired after the overnight train journey, and my aunt's declaration induced in me an intense desire to sleep. But at that precise moment, Aunt Anna announced that we had arrived at our destination. We set off for the long walk to her home. The first part was uphill, and I felt as if my legs were going to buckle under me. The long walk downhill was a lot easier. I just manage the flight of stairs leading up to the flat. By then I was staggering, and explained it by saying, that after a 24-hour train journey I felt that I was still in a moving vehicle. An explanation everybody accepted.

The downstairs neighbour came in with her small girl, just as my aunt was brewing a pot of tea. Louisa Miller seemed like a much younger woman than my aunt. Her mouth was not slanted downward but always seemed to be waiting for a chance to smile. Little Lynette had a contagious gaiety. Her laughter had the tone of jolly little bells. I took to the pair at once, and immediately the prospect of lodging with them made my family's apparent rejection seem less awful.

For what was left of the day I just managed to keep awake and conscious. Neighbours came in to gape at me. I realised through the fog of my exhaustion, that I was looked upon as a refugee from war torn France, not as a welcome family guest. By September 1946 the fighting in Normandy had been over for two years. The memory of the ordeal had been at last receding from my conscious mind. I had been looking forward to the future. The insistent questioning, threw me back into the nightmares of the allies' invasion.

The 1944 summer was again real, and that first night I screamed in my sleep, just as I had during the liberation. But the reaction I had from Louisa Miller was so different from the one I had experienced as a younger child, two years earlier. Louisa took me in her arms, and stayed with me until I was ready to go back to sleep. This act of kindness, she had to repeat several times in the ensuing weeks. It took quite a while for the nightmares to stop. My bad nights were in large part due to the endless repetition of the experiences I had gone through during the latest part of the war. All the visitors to my aunt's home demanded the story; it was the same scenario if we went on a visit. I had to sing for the box of chocolate or the second hand clothes I was given. Inevitably, every time the end of my story had a Swiss epilogue, and it was always the same. Those Swiss people also knew about bombardments; a lost bomb had fallen one night on the station of an important railway station in the canton.

One unfortunate result of my nightmares was that they contributed to the general attitude towards me. I was deemed to be a pathetic child, who had been saved from post-war France by the charity of her aunt. Every time she bought me a new garment, or a pair of shoes, I was made to go round the neighbourhood and show the purchases to all and sundry. The worst example of this was when new glasses were prescribed for me. I felt so humiliated by the experience that I would have almost preferred to go on twitching my nose to hitch up the pair the nuns had given me, despite the fact that they were too big for my face. I hated hearing the comments about the probable cost of these splendid spectacles.

My aunt's husband Uncle Pierre was a quiet man with a severe stammer, who spent much time humouring his spouse. His son, by his previous marriage was one month younger than me. Pierrot hated my aunt, who had changed his regime of eating what he liked, and going to bed when he felt ready, to a way of life she considered healthier for him. By extension, he took a dislike to me, associating me with his pet hate. It would have been too risky for him to take his resentment out on my aunt's pampered only son, Janot, who was older than us, and a perfect angel in his mother's eyes.

We went on foot to visit my mother's youngest sister. Aunt Theresa was married to a miller, and they lived in a house adjoining their flourmill. On the walk there, Aunt Anna told me that we would also meet my grandmother who lived nearby. According to Aunt Anna, she spent most of her days at the mill. I was terrified at the thought of meeting her. My early childhood had been full of my mother's tales about her hated parent, whom she said had never liked her. In the event the meeting with both my women relatives was cordial; although devoid of the outpouring of emotion, Aunt Anna had shown on seeing me for the first time. We sat in a dingy kitchen, where the proximity of the mill caused every surface to be covered with a fine layer of white dust. My jovial Uncle Amos came to meet me, he was also white from head to toe. After a large cup of tea, bread and delicious local gruyere cheese we went on our way. I remember feeling surprised and relieved; I had survived what I had feared would be a dreadful ordeal.

Chapter Two

My defects as a niece and granddaughter soon started to appear, and to be overtly criticised. I could not cook, was hopeless at housework, not much use with mending clothes and worst of all, I held my needles the wrong way when knitting. My mother, a great knitter, had taught me this skill. It had been the only craft I had enjoyed. While prisoner at the orphanage, I used to search for odd balls of wool on my visits home. If papa gave me some pocket money, I spent it on more knitting yarn. As I always finished my homework quickly, I knitted under my desk, woolly hats, scarves, mittens in a flash of multitude of colours. While we were not allowed to wear these garments in chapel or in town, the nuns tolerated them in the playground. But my aunt was much exercised by the way I held my needles and wool. She was determined to correct what she considered a perverted French way of knitting. She criticised my mother for unlearning the correct Swiss technique, the three sisters had been taught as children, and falling into bad habits. The result of this incessant nagging and shaming often in front of neighbours was that I took a violent dislike to the craft. I felt unable to convert easily to this new way of doing it, after years of handling wool and needles in a different manner. My fingers went on a guerrilla warfare with the needles, in which alternated go slows and downright sabotage of the work.

It was not only my lack of practical skills, which were exercising my aunt. Once the first flash of sentimentality had passed, almost everything about my person seemed to be an irritant. My French accent, the length of my skirts, my religion, my passion for reading and a newly acquired defect of severe clumsiness.

I did not speak French correctly, as in her view the Vaudois dialect was the only correct way to speak. When she sent me to "reduce" a room I did not know what she meant. I stood there for a moment, and returned to the kitchen. Later on when my aunt checked that I had done a good job, she came back angry because I had not done what she asked. But how was I to know that to "reduce" a room was to tidy it up.

I had very few clothes when I arrived, but my favourite dress was one my step -mother had ordered for me from a local dressmaker. The design was too young for me. I had wanted a dress with smocks for a long time, and I had been allowed it. My aunt thought the dress looked silly on a thirteen-year-old girl, which was true. She bought black cotton materials, one length with little blue flowers and the other with red designs. She asked Louisa Miller to make me overalls. Not wanting to vex my aunt, she did as she was bidden. She enlivened the garments with colourful rickrack at her own expense. Neither of my aunts had any experience of bringing up a girl. They dressed me, as if I too was a middle-aged country woman. When we went to a big department store in Lausanne, my aunt bought me a red tartan gathered skirt and a matching long sleeved blouse. I felt that I looked awful in this outfit. What I would have liked was a grey or navy pleated skirt, and a quiet blouse. I had always hated red. As a very young child, I had been wearing an overall of that colour while on a holiday on a farm. A ram had run after me, terrifying the five-year-old child that I was into an hysterical fit. The farmer told me it was my fault for wearing red, as it excited rams, just like bulls. But I had not chosen to wear red that day. The injustice made me sob all the louder. The farmer in his exasperation, decided to put me to bed until I had calmed down. He started to undress me, and I bit him on the arm to get him to stop, so he slapped me. The following Sunday, my parents came on a visit to see how I was settling. The farmer and his wife recounted my misdeeds. On hearing this I left the room quietly, gathered up my belongings and went to sit in the car. When leaving the farm, my parents tried calling me to take leave. I kept very quiet. I heard my mother say " well, if she won't show herself, let us go home". On seeing me in the car she was furious, but papa said that if I did not enjoy the holiday, I might as well leave. My mother was reluctant to let me have my way. But I was holding on to the seat with all my strength, she had to agree to take me home. I always associated wearing red with an unpleasant experience, and would never choose clothes of this colour.

Every Sunday when returning from church, I was greeted by a torrent of recriminations. It so happened that the only Catholic mass in this Protestant village, ended at the time my aunt was busy cooking the most important meal of the week: Sunday lunch. My defect was that I was not there to help her. I had not planned it that way. That is how it was. I was also bearing the brunt of my aunt's resentment towards my mother's conversion to Catholicism, which the family could not condone. Her relatives were not to know that it had been a conversion of convenience, which had not come from the heart but from the head. It was the only way my mother and papa could have a religious wedding; my mother having been brought up a Protestant. I could only remember my mother going to church twice from the date of this marriage, until her death a few years later. But I had left the orphanage, and its heavy indoctrination only a couple of months earlier. Despite my shaky faith, I was not yet prepared to take the risk of eternal damnation. The Catholic girls my own age were a friendly little crowd. It was very pleasant to stroll gently home after mass. I enjoyed the relaxed interlude with them, while putting off the return to the house. My religion contributed to the schism between my family and I.

The greatest source of the irritation I caused the entire family, was certainly my passion for books. I had enjoyed reading since I was a young child. My mother thought that toys were bad for the character. She never bought me any. The only dolls I had a as child were gifts from outsiders, who felt sorry for me. Even the nursery school had put a doll in a sewing basket, which my mother insisted I ask from Father Christmas. She provided me with books before I could even read fluently. I also had plenty of coloured crayons, drawing material and anything she considered educational. I lost my ability to draw early, but my thirst for reading material only increased as I grew older, and was more able to decipher complex texts. I had to read; I needed to read; I could not live without it. If deprived of books, I would read anything I could lay my eyes on. There was no room for books in my aunt's house, and I was not allowed to borrow any from friends. So I read my uncle's newspapers from cover to cover, including all the small adverts, boring as they were. I perused the catalogues of the big mail order firms over and over again. I drove my aunt almost crazy with frustration. All she wanted me to be was a good little Swiss Ms, knitting, sewing, dusting furniture, and three times a day washing the kitchen floor. While I never refused to help with the chores, it was always with an eye towards the escape route of the next piece of written words. Aunt Anna engaged the cooperation of my grand mother and Aunt Theresa, in a desperate attempt to cure me of this useless passion. Aunt Theresa did not have much to say. But my grand mother was lyrical on the subject of husbands who left their wives, because they spent the day reading books instead of attending to the household chores. Often neglecting to cook for their spouses. I told her that I had no intention of ever getting married, so this would not happen to me. The big question which the family asked, and which I could not answer to their satisfaction was "when you have read a book what have you got to show for it?" I could hear my aunt telling people how useless I was. I often saw the commiseration in the faces of the women.

The only person who took no notice of these criticisms was Louisa, perhaps because she too had a useless passion. She was a wireless fanatic. I discovered this one evening. I had gone down to her flat earlier than usual. Radio Sottens was wonderful, and inspired in me a lifelong love of the medium. I enjoyed the talks, the music and above all the plays. The first one I listened to was a dramatisation of Daphne du Maurier's " REBECCA". I was hooked for life. Needless to say, my family was against the wireless; it was qualified as the kind of frivolity Louisa would indulge in. So I had to box clever, if I wanted to indulge in another unproductive activity. I began to plead tiredness and bid the family an early good night, the evening's plays were broadcasted. There was always a certain tension in the air, while I listened to the plays with Louisa. My aunt occasionally came down to have a chat with her in the evening. Sometimes, I had to make a dash for my bed, if we heard someone coming down the stairs. When Louisa's husband was present he joined in the conspiracy. Jacques was the prompter at the local amateur dramatic group, and so was often out in the evenings. But if he was at home, he treated the tricking of my aunt as a huge joke. I stayed up rather late on the evenings of the broadcasts, and consequently woke up later the following mornings. My aunt complained about that too.

Chapter Three

When I first arrived in Switzerland, my aunt started the formalities to have me admitted to the local school. But as with all Vaudois decisions, this one took some time. When the letter finally arrived, I had already fallen from grace. However, the family thought that as I was not going to be in the academic stream, but in a more down to earth class it may do me good. The course I joined included the teaching of some domestic skills for the girls. The boys enjoyed lessons in citizenship, which were considered unsuitable for the female gender. The class master, Mr Audon, was generally quite tough with the pupils, but he never showed me anything but kindness. When I was afflicted by a dreadful cough, he even gave me lozenges to help relieve it. Of course, the rather mixed bunch of adolescents in the class enjoyed teasing me about it in a rather crude way, which I could not always fully understand. I was not familiar with the juvenile sexual slang fashionable at the time.

The needlework mistress had no time for me. She told me quite bluntly that as I was not going to take the end of year examinations, she was not prepared to waste time helping me with my work. So I was left to dream the afternoons away. I enjoyed listening to the romantic novels, which were read out loud by a pupil in an attempt to keep the noise level down. These novels often had English characters in them. As the pupils in the lower stream had no knowledge of the English language, some curious pronunciation often took place. For example, Lady Orietta was said to be " laddie" Orietta. As I knew no better myself at the time, this error did not diminish my pleasure. It was such a refreshing change from the life of the saint martyrs, which I had to endure at the orphanage.

A more unfortunate result of my going to school was that I frequently overheard the other children talking about their parents in a way that was anything but respectful. They often repeated parts of the conversational exchanges that were supposed to be taking place in their home. This gave me the idea that perhaps I was too docile with my family. I decided that I should try to stand my ground more when I was in opposition to my aunt. I had survived so far by being mostly passive, and by the use of a certain amount of underhand trickery. The first show down took place when winter came. I was given one of my boy cousin's cast off coat to wear. I bluntly refused, saying I wanted a girl's coat. Aunt Anna was very upset, but adamant. I was to wear this coat or go without, which I did for a while. The Swiss winter was closing in, and going off to school in the early mornings I felt very cold. It was left to Louisa, to point out to me that the coat was made so it could be worn by children of both genders, as it buttoned equally on the left or on the right. I then agreed to wear it. On our next visit to the mill, Aunt Anna complained to the rest of the family. I was no longer the nice little girl who had arrived a few months earlier. Aunt Theresa replied that I was a little *"crapaude"*.

The only moment I was able to give the family any kind of satisfaction, was at meal times. When I first arrived, they were anxious that being used to the French cuisine, I would not care for the Swiss diet. The well-fed Swiss, had very little idea of the near starvation regime with which we had to survive during the war years. Perhaps, because Aunt Helene was such an accomplished cook, from day one I could never have enough. It must have been a blend of enjoying her excellent cuisine, and of having at last enough to eat after years of privation. For once, the whole family approved of me. While complaining about my numerous inadequacies to all who would listen, Aunt Anna would end her diatribe by saying. "At least she is easy to feed, the only dish she is not keen on is fondue". Though she berated Pierrot on occasions for his greediness, the more I ate the happier she was. This did not endear me to him, as he felt treated unfairly by her. He kept trying to get me into trouble and on one occasion, he succeeded.

We were both in the same class at the school where he was an indifferent scholar. One day, I had let drop a crayon on the floor. When I bent down to retrieve it, I could not avoid seeing that the boy sitting immediately behind me had dropped his trousers, and thus exposed his full genitalia. I pretended not to have noticed. But when we returned home Pierrot told my aunt. In her fury, she insisted that I report the incident to the master, or leave the school. I was thus forced to speak to the teacher the following morning. Poor Mr Audon looked even more embarrassed than I was. The boy was punished at once, and the facts reported to the school commission. The whole affair was blown out of all proportion to the deed. After that, nearly the whole class sent me to Coventry. Pierrot never owned up to having reported the affair to my aunt, so they all blamed me. Even the girls thought that I had been very childish, which upset me greatly.

But despite the unfairness of my classmates about the incident in the schoolroom, the girls were near the truth by referring to my inherent childishness. I had nurtured the idea that being in Switzerland, at last with my real family, I could catch up on the childhood I never had. I had survived the years of depravation, sustained by the idea that one day, I would have a happy childhood. I had totally failed to understand that it would not be possible. I was nearly 14 years old so it was too late for me to be a little girl. But it is what I wanted. It was why I had asked my stepmother for a dress with smocks, and why I needed cuddles all the time. I certainly was not getting my craving for demonstrative affection satisfied by the family. Aunt Anna's way of caring was practical; my physical needs were very well met. It was downstairs with the Millers that I regressed and enjoyed being cuddled. I was tucked up in bed and kissed good night by Louisa and Jacques. Sleeping in a room with a two-year-old little girl, facilitated the acting out of my fantasy. With the Millers I was an affectionate little girl. Upstairs my family endured a reluctant adolescent. This split made it well nigh impossible for me to settle as part of the family, engaged as we all were in a dialogue of the deaf.

I did not fare much better at the mill. Aunt Theresa had two grown-up sons, and a third son, who was a couple of years younger than me. She was not overtly unkind to me, just indifferent. As for my grand mother, she was totally absorbed in her relationship with the little boy, Claude. The two of them behaved like a pair of lovesick sweethearts. The whole family laughed about it behind their back. But of course, no one set about rescuing the child. Until my arrival in Switzerland, there was no grand daughter for my grand mother to enjoy. When I arrived, I was too old, and in any case the pattern with Claude was well established. One day on a visit to the mill, my grand mother handed me a few coins saying, "here you are, five francs for you, I gave 10 francs to Claude". I was not a mercenary child but the remark told me where I stood in the family's pecking order. I was not to forget it, nor to forgive it.

It was a hard reality that my grandmother had disliked my mother. Despite her daughter's early death, the old woman never had a sympathetic or indulgent word to say about her. She seemed to enjoy telling me, all the things my mother had been unable to perform to the family's satisfaction. When I expressed the wish to learn to ride a bicycle, my grandmother joined Aunt Anna in saying that clumsy as I was, I would probably be like my mother. I would fall all over the place, which of course, I did. And it was not just off the bicycle that I was falling. I had become so nervous that I seemed to be unable to stay on my feet. At home, I crashed in the corridor, sustaining a cut lip and severe nosebleed. What was even worse, I soiled the wall with my blood. I fell on my back coming out of church, dirtying my unisex coat. Once arriving just in time at school, I tripped and ended up on my knees. This fall made two big holes, in the woolly stockings Aunt Helene had just finished knitting. It all added up to convincing the family that I was a useless, hopeless girl, who did not even like them. Before long, there came the decision that they must get rid of me.

An apparently banal incident was the drop that made the glass of my inadequacies overspill. One morning my aunt sent me to borrow a cooking ingredient from Louisa. Instead of coming back quickly, I lingered downstairs for nearly an hour. When I returned my aunt was crying with rage. She announced that she had had enough. She was not going to make an application for my visa to be renewed, and in a few weeks I would be back to France. When she had calmed down, she said that I could write to papa that my visa had been refused, so as to save my face. That was the story she told everyone outside the family, to save hers.

Chapter Four

On my arrival in Normandy, the content of my suitcases received a warm welcome. My aunt had made sure. I went back to France with a good supply of clothes and footwear. I had barely opened my luggage, than my stepmother Justine tried on every garment. She decided that I was to share my little trousseau with her. She did not ask my opinion, but took for her own use all the garments she liked and which fitted her. This included some fine embroidered lawn cotton chemises. Luckily, she could not get her feet into my shoes, which saved me the loss of them. I did not protest at her riffling through my cases, so frightened was I of her temper. Despite my inner resentment, I even applauded when a garment really suited her. But my repressed fury got the better of my cowardice. One day, Justine was singing a silly song about farm animals having taken over a house. When she got to the couplet, "I went to the bedroom where the cow was changing her chemise", I exclaimed with some feeling, "The cow was very lucky, I brought back some chemises, so she could have one to change into". My stepmother's reaction was violent; she locked me in a room until papa came home. He was drunk, and very angry. He demanded that I apologise to his wife before he let me out. This was the end of the very brief honeymoon, I had enjoyed with them.

Justine was disappointed that my Swiss family had not offered to send regular money for my keep. Both of my parents made it quite clear, they had no intention of letting me resume my education.

They had decided to find me some paid employment. I had celebrated my fourteenth birthday only four months earlier and the last thing I wanted, was to be pushed into manual work. My ambitions were to study law and literature. Even this had been a realistic compromise by me. I had wanted with all my heart to be a classical actress. However, having seen films in which beautiful women like Michèle Morgan and Danielle Darrieu appeared, I had given up the ambition of playing Moliere at the Comedy Française. I thought I was too plain. I had realised this while in Switzerland. I had heard many people, who had known my mother, say, "you look like your mama but she was beautiful".

Chapter Five

The Chaplain of the orphanage sent a message asking to see me. When I arrived, he immediately wanted to know what plans had been made for my future. I told him that the family's poverty necessitated that I start work as soon as possible. He then offered to pay for my studies, and support me financially as long as my education lasted. I was overjoyed, and ran home with the news of his amazing generosity. Papa and Justine's first question was to ask me how old Father Renouf was. I was not too sure, but I said I thought he was quite elderly. My parents' reaction was that I should accept the money, and start my studies. But should the old priest die before I finish my education, I would leave college at once and take up employment. They then could pocket the rest of the funds, for the benefit of the whole family. I felt so ashamed that I could not bring myself to tell the kind old man what had been said. I told him instead that I was not interested in returning to school. I could see that I had severely disappointed him.

A few weeks later a messenger was sent from the orphanage to inform me that the Father had died suddenly. He was 76 years old and had suffered a cerebral haemorrhage. I went to see him in the little house where he had so generously given of himself to " little Clara ". When I walked into the room, a few drops of blood ran down one of his nostrils. This upset me greatly, as everyone in the room turned their eyes towards me. The nuns present seemed to think I had something to do with the nosebleed. They said that Father Renouf had been very worried about me. I was very upset, but I could not feel guilty. I felt that I had done my best to protect him from the cupidity of my family.

When I returned home papa was drunk. Egged on by Justine, he badgered me about refusing the old man's money. He thought that if it had not been for my stupidity, they would be rich now.

The atmosphere in the house became very tense. Justine never missed a chance to tell me what a burden I was. I listened to it all silently, but the day she told me I ate too much, I simply stopped eating. I survived on water, and a few lumps of sugar. I took them out of the cupboard when my parents were out. It was amazing that after a few days, I stopped having hunger pangs. I rather enjoyed the feeling of light-headedness, which made me think I was floating. It took papa and Justine two weeks to comment on my lack of appetite. I invented an abdominal pain, and Justine took me to see the family physician.

After an examination, during which I was unable to tell the doctor where exactly my non-existent pain was located, he asked Justine to return to the waiting room. As soon as she was out of earshot, he pressed me gently to explain to him what was really worrying me. The kindness in this voice was just too much for me; I burst into tears. When I had calmed down, I told him the whole story. He was very sympathetic, but explained that I could not keep to the fasting any longer. He promised to help me out of the impasse, I found myself in. In return, I should give him my word that I would do as he asked, which I did. He called Justine, and told her that with medication I would soon be well. He also suggested a light diet for a few days, after which I should be able to resume a normal fare. After refusing to take Justine's money, he escorted us to the door, putting his hand lightly on my shoulder as we left.

Chapter Six

A year and a half later, I found myself again on the train to Paris, on my way to Switzerland. For over a year I had worked in a hotel, as a skivvy. My wages were taken from me every week by my father, and spent in the nearest bar. He usually returned mid-week, and asked me to hand over my tips. These, too, were used to calm his unquenchable thirst. The cash I succeeded in hiding from him could not be used to buy myself clothing or footwear, let alone books. So I spent it on cinema tickets and patisseries. In my two free afternoons, I gorged myself with chocolate éclairs and choux à la crème, before taking refuge in the darkness of a cinema.

When it was at last arranged that I should sleep at the hotel, I was able to buy books. I read them in the broom cupboard, which had been transformed into a bedroom for my use. It had no window, so the air always smelled stale. The total absence of daylight was almost compensated by the great advantage of having a private corner. The main problem was that the hotel owner could see under the door, if I was using electricity. I had to buy candles to supplement my torch, when I ran out of batteries. The snag with the candles was that it was rather dangerous to read under the sheets. I had a couple of near misses, when I almost set the bed on fire. After that I was very careful. I did not stop using the candles, but I held them well away from the bed linen. I had to keep an ear switched to the noise on the landing, in case Madame saw the light under the door.

Madame Lebrun was not a cruel woman, but she ran this small family hotel with no skilled help. She not only worked very hard herself, but expected the same level of application from the small staff. Most of the residents were North African workers. They had come to Avranches to clear up the bombsites and start the rebuilding of the town. As they worked locally, they took their three daily meals at the hotel. Madame Lebrun did all the cooking.

Every morning, at six thirty, a loud bang on the door woke me up. Within minutes, I was downstairs to help serve the boarders' breakfast. When I had washed up the crockery, I cleaned the bedrooms of the residents, and the accommodation used by the passing trade. This was followed by a speedy return to the kitchen. I peeled and cleaned the huge quantity of vegetables and salad, needed for both lunch and the evening meal. While the lady cooked, I laid the tables. Then I helped serve the meal, cleared up the tables and washed up in preparation for supper. If I was finished early, then I might have had a short break in the afternoon. Then I restarted the whole cycle in the evening.

On market days, or if there was a banquet, additional help was at hand in the form of a woman who would be serving the meals. I was glued for several hours to the kitchen sink, washing up. I had no other help to wash off the grease from the crockery, than a handful of soda crystals. My hands were often red raw, due to the harshness of these salts. On the evening before market day, all the vegetables and salads had to be prepared. There would be no time to do this in the morning. I used to be very tired after the short night's sleep. Occasionally, I dropped the left over food into the washing up water, and the crockery in the rubbish bin.

I was only fourteen years old, when I started work at the hotel. After nearly a year of this punishing schedule, my health broke down. I had pigeon size eggs on my neck, axilla and groin. I could not complain of any specific pain, it seems that I just folded up. All I wanted to do was sleep. I did not particularly want to go back home since at the hotel I was well fed and left in peace. But Madame Lebrun made me realise that it was all too much for her. She could not cope without a maid, and I was giving her work. So I went home.

Justine was not very pleased to see me. She told me that I was listening to myself, which was her way of saying that I was being self-indulgent. When I showed her the enlarged glands on my body she promptly put me to bed and called the family doctor. Until he had seen me, she kept her baby away from my room, lest what I had should be contagious. She would not even touch the clothes I had just discarded.

The doctor asked me how I had occupied my time since I had last seen him over a year ago. I began telling him that I worked at the hotel. I was quickly interrupted by Justine, who said, in laughter, that running a few errands hardly qualified as work. According to her, I spent most of my time playing with her baby.

The doctor and Justine left the room, and carried on the conversation behind the door. After a while, I tiptoed near the partition. I overheard Justine asking the doctor if he thought that in view of the way my mother had died, I could be a degenerate. The doctor replied firmly that there could be no connection between my mother's illness, and my depleted state. I rushed back to bed, filled with impotent rage towards Justine. I could do nothing to escape her power. The gloom, which had tainted everything for me since the previous summer was at that moment overpowering.

When my health improved, Justine decided that I would not go back to the hotel. A neighbour had told her that a noble family living locally was looking for a maid.

My stepmother took me to be presented to Mademoiselle de... I was engaged on the strength of a five-minute interview, all of us standing in the kitchen. I felt desperate, as during my convalescence I had restarted dreaming that I may at last be allowed to go back to school. For one brief moment, I thought I might escape the dreadful fate that awaited me. This was when Justine discussed my wages with Mademoiselle de.... She was not objecting to the amount offered, but to the lady's insistence that I should receive my dues monthly. My stepmother had demanded that I should be paid weekly. Mademoiselle won the contest because as she said. "Cela ne se fait pas dans les bonnes maisons, de payer les domestiques chaque semaine". My stepmother, who was obviously visiting a grand house for the first time, did not know any better. A little humiliated, she capitulated.

Papa was not too pleased to hear that he was going to lose his regular cider and Calvados money. However, he was relieved that I was going to be resident in that grand house. I would cost nothing to the family.

Papa had lost his part of the partnership of the transport firm, which he had founded with his brother before the war. He had survived doing casual work which paid badly, and which also proved insecure. At last, he found permanent full-time work with a funeral company in Avranches. But the situations he had to deal with very often upset him. So he drank even more than usual. He would drink after work was finished. But now he began to get rather drunk before doing the job, and soon lost the post.

What income I could bring to the household was very important to Justine. She knew that papa would never dare go to the grand house to collect my wages. He would instead, use even more of his own income to finance his drinking. Papa was obviously not too pleased about that. His wife had for the first time, an idea of the amount of money he spent on alcohol. Justine, having been brought up on Normandy farms, accepted that the cider pitcher and the Calvados decanter were never off the kitchen table. She did not seem to be overtly concerned at that time by her husband's alcoholism. The euphemism used to refer to the state in which he came in at night, was that the poor man was tired. If he vomited everywhere, he was obviously ill.

Justine's main concern was the lack of money, stuck as she was at home with her second baby. They had lost the little girl, born from the pregnancy, which had precipitated her marriage to papa. Claudia died when she was nearly a year old. This remarkable little girl walked at nine months and talked in whole sentences by the time she died. She had caught whooping cough. Her mother refused her antibiotics. This was because the child next door had died having convulsions, after the administration of such treatment. I was only twelve years old at the time, but even at that age I could not understand my stepmother. She chose what she called a beautiful death for her baby, rather than do her utmost to save her.

The second baby was born nine months after the death of little Claudia. Jocelyne was altogether a different sort of child. She took her time learning to sit, walk and talk. Like Claudia, she had inherited the Cobin good looks, and she was very sweet tempered.

The only regular income finding its way directly into Justine's pocket was the family allowance she was getting for two children. The authorities were unaware of my six-month stay in Switzerland, or my full time work at the hotel.

Justine was anxious that I should take up my post at the de... as soon as possible. I arrived at the grand house early one Monday morning. I was ushered in by the cleaner, who was on her way out. Mademoiselle de... introduced me to her mother, the old Countess, then to the Count who was senile and never left his room. The only manifestation of his presence was a continual loud-moaning, which was audible all over the house. This noise was very unnerving; it could only be avoided by shutting the kitchen door. But every time Mademoiselle came into the kitchen, she left the door open on her way out. It was also the habit of the fourth member of the family; a little girl of eight, who was living with her aunt and grandparents. On meeting the child, I was informed that I should address her as Mademoiselle Benedicte. I was fifteen years old and could not bring myself to calling a young child Mademoiselle, so I avoided calling her anything.

I seemed to spend most of my time in the kitchen preparing food. After the meals, I washed up the delicate china, and kept the silver sparkling. All the family meals were taken in style, even the only cup of coffee Mademoiselle had for breakfast, must be presented correctly. The old Countess never came into the kitchen. Mademoiselle de... hovered during the preparation of the meals. She told me, step by step, what I should do, if I told her something was new to me. She invariably, put the final touch to the dishes, adding cream to one, making a sauce for another.

I ate my meals in the kitchen, on the corner of the table where the dirty crockery was piled up. There was usually enough food left over for me. However, the dishes, which came back from the dining room were so messy, that I soon lost my appetite. The only meal I could swallow was breakfast: the French tradition of "café au lait" and buttered bread did not create havoc in the kitchen.

My room was under the eaves. It had no heating, running water or sanitation. In the notoriously cold January of 1948, I was so cold that I slept fully clothed. I supplemented the two thin blankets provided, by spreading on the bed the few garments I had brought from home. Rather than break the ice in the water jug in the morning, I did not wash. My only toilet consisted of pushing a comb through my hair. I emptied the chamber pot through the dormer window. The content rolled into the guttering that hemmed the roof. Thus I avoided most nights doing the journey two floors below to use the lavatory. I was seen by Mademoiselle one night when the needs of nature had forced me to go downstairs. On seeing me fully clothed, she assumed that I had got up too early She sent me back to bed, with even a hint of kindness in her voice. But by morning the slave-mistress relationship was resumed. I noticed it when I tried to give her a cheery "good morning Madam" which was met by a blank face.

On market days in Avranches, the farmers from the surrounding countryside came to town to sell their goods. So when I answered the bell, I was not surprised to be confronted by a jolly farmer carrying a huge basket full of farm produce. I went back to the kitchen and told Mademoiselle that there was a gentleman at the door. She said sharply, "well, take him to the drawing room". So I went back and told the farmer to follow me. He protested, asking me if I was sure that was right. I said, "yes, that is what Mademoiselle said". So he did as asked but remained standing in the middle of the room. Within a few seconds I heard raised voices coming from the drawing room. In the next instance, the farmer was in the kitchen depositing his wares. When he was gone, the lady said to me very angrily, "you are old enough to know the difference between a man and a gentleman". I was devastated but I was not going to let this woman see me cry, so I swallowed my sobs.

The next day being Sunday, I was allowed the rest of the day off after I had cleared up the midday meal. Not having the means to buy a cinema ticket or patisseries, I went home. The front door was opened. I stood at the entrance for an instance, getting ready to face my stepmother. On seeing me, Justine asked how things were going. All the humiliation and thorough hopelessness of the week came over me. I dissolved in uncontrollable sobs. Surprisingly, she said, "you do not have to go back". Justine arranged for the neighbour who had recommended the job to tell the de... that I was not going to return.

A few days later I had to go back to the grand house to collect my meagre belongings. Mademoiselle followed me to my former bedroom, and watched what I was packing. She asked me why I had not hung my spare clothes in the cupboard provided. I told her that I had needed them on the bed to keep warm. All she said was that the other servants had not complained of the cold. I said quietly, "neither did I".

As I was leaving the house, she asked me if I could tell her what had displeased me in the post. From the height of my 15 years, all I could think of replying was, "No madam, because you could never understand".

Chapter Seven

Soon after that the beatings started. Justine had decided that she would go out to work. I was left to do the housework, cook the midday meal and look after her little girl. But I could not be motivated to do much in the house. Most mornings, I spent hours sitting by the stove, with the baby on my lap. I was gorging her with "petit beurre biscuits" which she loved, while I read the daily newspapers from cover to cover. The baby was happy and so was I; but her mother was not. If the house was not spotlessly clean when she came home, there would be a scene of operatic proportions. I just about managed to cook the meal when there was food in the house. However, most days my stepmother had to be paid for her morning's work, to be able to buy the food for the day. When papa came home for his lunch, he was more than half full of cider and Calvados. His wife's complaints would make him very angry. The two of them would launch a physical attack on me. I would put my hands over my head, so my arms received most of the slaps. But there was nothing I could do to protect my backside from the kicks.

When papa came home in the evenings, he was usually very drunk. He always had a reason to abuse me verbally or physically. His trick was to ask me what I thought of a certain item of news. Whatever I gave him as a reply was his excuse to launch at me. I began to say I knew nothing of the matter he wished to discuss. This infuriated him even more. Sometimes he put the carving knife at my throat, saying I should not be allowed to live. He was convinced that what he called my superior education had made me arrogant. In my braver moods, I would snigger that I had hardly enjoyed that at the orphanage. Justine was convinced that it was the months I had spent in Switzerland, which had given me ideas of grandeur.

Her anger with the Swiss did not stop her from raiding the parcels that were sent by my aunt. I was also ordered periodically to use my so-called bad health to write begging letters to my family. When the cash came, I was never lucky enough to catch the postman. I did not benefit from these small windfalls, which were soon converted into liquid benefit for papa. If Justine was able to get the letter first, she would hide the money from him. For a few days she would be quite nice to me. She needed my signature on the money order, and my promises of silence.

After the Second World War, France was very short of skilled craftsmen. In 1948, the government announced that an enhanced family allowance would be paid to families, which had a youngster engaged in a bona fide apprenticeship. Justine set about scouring the town to find me such a post. Anything would do, so long as it fulfilled the official criteria. I was so upset by this idea that I could neither eat nor sleep. She searched the town looking for a suitable employer. In that event I was lucky, as she found a milliner, who was keen to get involved in the scheme. Notwithstanding my clumsiness with a needle, it was so much better than what I anticipated. I was genuinely relieved. I had feared that my parents would place me in a butcher's shop, or in an agricultural setting, which they often threatened to do.

The milliner's workshop was a little corner of paradise at the back of the showroom. It was quite small, and I liked its cosiness. A mother and daughter ran the enterprise. Madame Saufron received the clients and manned the till. The daughter Denise was responsible for the interpretation of the client's wishes and their creation. A number of hats were displayed in the shop window so as to entice the ladies of the town. We also saw a large number of the women who came to Avranches on market days. Situated as the shop was at the very edge of the market place, the sight of it could not be avoided by shoppers. The combination of this situation, and Denise's talent as a milliner could not fail to make it a success.

I was instantly accepted by the two women. It was not taken for granted that I was useless with my hands, and so I proved quickly that I was not. Every time I learned a new technique, Denise would call to her mother, "Clara is so smart". Without getting up from the till, Madame Saufron would reply, "of course" or "I know". After a little while Denise and I would mouth quietly the comment we were expecting, and try hard to suppress our fits of giggles when we got the correct one.

I enjoyed contributing to making elegant hats, and not only because of their inherent beauty. The endless variety of the creations awakened in me a need I had not known was there. That was the craving to try endlessly to achieve something better.

On quiet days in the shop, Madame would disappear for some hours and Denise and I talked. When the warm weather came, she discovered my bruised arms. So relieved was I to have someone to confide in that I told her the truth about my situation. The beatings had not only continued, but were getting worse.

The shop was about ten minutes on foot from our house so I went home for a lunch, which Justine had prepared. I was expected to clear up after the meal before going back to work. Most days that worked well. It was my responsibility to cook the evening meal on my return from the workshop. Sometimes a client would linger, and we shut the showroom a few minutes late. I would be accused of having picked men up on my way home. I was called a whore by papa and Justine, and received more severe abuse than the normal daily dose. If papa were not at home when I arrived, Justine would throw in a vicious remark about my inevitable likeness to my mother. She never dared abuse the memory of my mother when papa was there. He seldom talked about his first wife, but when he did it was always to remember her numerous talents. Whether it was her ability to turn a simple dish into a delicacy, or her musically entrancing voice. Everything about her was in his eyes exceptional. Justine would get out of his earshot, and murmur between her teeth "Yes, but she was a whore".

The success I was enjoying at work began to have an effect on my behaviour at home. I became bolder in my dealings with Justine. I answered her taunts in a very provoking manner. One day my stepmother was going on about my superior education, I said to her. "The main difference between our education is that I received mine sitting at a desk in a classroom, you got yours sitting on a stool at the backside of cows". It was only time I saw her burst into tears, but when papa came home he made me ask her forgiveness on my knees.

The end came very suddenly. On market days, I did not go home for lunch. Madame Saufron often sent me to buy buckwheat galettes for the three of us at a stall in the square. One Saturday, I met my godmother who was also queuing up for this local speciality. She offered to take me to the cinema the following day. I told her that I would not be allowed to go to the evening screening, and she settled for the matinee. In the middle of the film the projector broke down, and it took some time for it to be repaired. Inevitably the show finished later than advertised. It was well after the time I should have been home to prepare the evening meal. I told my god-mother that I was too frightened to go home, so she decided to accompany me. When we reached the house papa was very drunk, and Justine in a raging temper. My godmother tried to explain about the projector, but her presence did not inhibit them. They both started to hit me. The next day my godmother came to the shop having brought with her paper, envelope and stamp. She advised me to write to the Swiss aunts, and tell them not to send any more money or clothes. I should explain that I did not benefit from their generosity.

The response from Switzerland came swiftly. I had written a begging letter only a few days before. Dictated by Justine, it was telling my aunt that my health did not permit me to work. Aunt Anna reacted sharply to having been tricked, while respecting my request of silence about the first letter. Her answer was that I should return to Switzerland, where my future would be assured. I took this to mean that I would be allowed to resume my education. Despite my sadness at leaving the workshop, I was quite elated.

When the money for my train tickets arrived, papa and Justine spent it. After several requests from my aunt to be given the date of my arrival, papa was forced to borrow my fare from his brother.

The day before my departure for Switzerland, I met a relative of Justine. I told her of my imminent journey. She immediately declared herself very relieved to hear my news. She told me that many people in the town were aware of the dreadful treatment I was enduring. I was appalled that no one had made a move to help me. I was instantly, overwhelmed by a violent and enduring resentment towards the people of Avranches.

Chapter Eight

I arrived at Vallorbe early in the morning, having travelled since the previous afternoon. I had been unable to sleep on the overnight train. This was the end of the summer. The carriage had been full of Italian seasonal workers, who were returning to their country. We were crammed on the seats, as tightly as cigarettes in a new pack. I had thought, that it was the smell of sweat and salamis that had made me feel rather sick. However, as soon as I got off the train, I realised that it was the prospect of meeting my family, which had knotted my guts.

I was expecting to be met by Aunt Anna, but she was not there. I barely recognised Marion, the young woman who greeted me. I had only met her a few times on my previous visit. While I was away, she had been hurriedly married to Janot when she was found to be pregnant. I was at first relieved that she was there. But if her attitude was a foretaste of what was awaiting me, on meeting the rest of the family, it did not bode well. Her first words were "you do not look very sick!" She was silent on the train journey to La Sarraz. As I sat looking at her closed face, my anxiety level rose to an unbearable pitch. The reception I had from Aunt Anna was barely friendly. She was more interested in pushing bits of soap up the anus of her constipated grandson, than eager to welcome me.

When she eventually found the time, she informed me that she had sworn after my first visit that she would never have me back, unless she could lodge me. Janot's marriage had forced her to change position. Louisa and her family had now moved into their new villa.

But the space they had occupied, was now needed for the young family. I was to be farmed out again. Much against her better judgement, she had asked Louisa if I could have a room in her new house. My grandmother and Aunt Theresa would pay the rent until other arrangements were made.

The first few evenings Aunt Anna took me to Louisa's home, a mere 10 minutes walk up the hill. I soon told her that despite the darkening evenings, I was not frightened. When she was accompanying me she lingered on. I so needed Louisa and Jacques all to myself. It was soon evident that the easygoing relationship the two women had enjoyed all their lives had become more formal. A kind of stiffness had seeped in their rapport. I wondered if the problem had been due to my behaviour during my previous stay. Louisa very quickly reassured me. Janot was the cause of the unease between them. My cousin worked at the blanket mill. A few months earlier, he had been caught having sexual intercourse with a mentally handicapped woman. This vulnerable person was employed to sweep the workshops. A workman reported the incident to Jacques Miller. He was the executive in charge of the unit. Because of the closeness of the two families, Jacques felt it to be very important that he should be seen to behave according to the strictest rules of the firm. This was a case, when a reprimand and a simple warning would not do. The report of the incident had been made at eleven o'clock, and fifteen minutes later Janot found himself on the road with his cards in his pocket. My aunt had been very upset at Jacques's failure to make an exception, and save Janot's job.

Newly married and with a baby due soon, he found himself unable to find a comparable post locally. He was reduced to doing unskilled work, for a local builder. When talking to Louisa, my aunt had likened that Jacques's behaviour and subsequent sacking of Janot, to what would have happened, if having seen little Lynette drowning, she had pushed her head under the water. Louisa understood my aunt's anxiety about her son's lack of prospect. However, she knew of old Anna's inability to have a realistic view of Janot.

During my first visit, I had become aware of Janot's sexual incontinence. A very pretty girl in my class was fostered in the care of a local farmer. She was attending school, as well as helping on the land. She told me how on her way home, she had been waylaid by Janot. He had tumbled her in a ditch. She had had great difficulty in freeing herself. She had been punished by the farmer's wife for dirtying her school clothes. I asked her why she had not told the lady what had happened to her. Her reply was that in Switzerland children in care counted for nothing, beyond being a source of cheap labour. "Beside", she said, "my lady is a friend of your aunt."

I had also occasions of having to deal personally with Janot's inappropriate behaviour. One day I was sitting at the kitchen table, absorbed in reading the newspaper. I came across an article, which caught my eye. I said out loud, "Oh! Isn't this interesting?" Janot, who was close by, said to me, "And this, isn't it interesting, too?" I turned round only to see his fully exposed genitalia. I left the kitchen, followed by the sound of his mocking laughter.

Shortly after, my aunt sent me to put away Janot's newly pressed laundry. He happened to be in his room. As I made for the door he pushed me violently on to his bed, and pressing on my chest with one hand he swiftly got the other one in my knickers. I was so shocked that it took me a few seconds to react, but I managed to free myself when he relaxed the hand, which was holding me down. This was just as he was trying to push a finger into my body. Without a word I ran out of the room. I found my aunt next door putting away her stepson's clean clothes. How could Janot behave thus in the close proximity of his mother? Louisa explained this clearly, when I told her about all these incidents. It was because he knew that if caught by Anna, I would be blamed. At the first opportunity, I had asked for her advice. What was the best way of informing my aunt of her son's behaviour. Her advice was to take measures to protect myself from Janot, but to say nothing to my aunt. She thought Aunt Anna would not believe me. She thought she might even say that poor Janot had been seduced by my school friend and I. Her reaction to his dismissal from the mill proved Louisa to have judged the situation only too accurately.

The two women had not fallen out over Janot's sacking. They were just uneasy together. My aunt appeared oblivious of the pain she had inflicted on Louisa and Jacques. How could she suggest that pushing little Lynette's head under water was equivalent to the loss of a job. The couple had been very hurt. They had lost a young baby some years earlier. Lynette had been a long time coming, after the bereavement. The little girl was their only, very precious child.

Chapter Nine

I had been waiting with a mixture of anxiety and relief, as I prepared to discuss with my aunt what the family situation had been in France. I felt that perhaps the time had at last come, when I could discuss openly my mother's behaviour during the German occupation. Also I needed to explain the chain of consequences ensuing from it. The burden of this secret had been crippling me for such a long time. I longed to put it down. During my first visit, I had stuck strictly to the official version that my mother had caught typhoid fever during an epidemic. Syphilis was never mentioned or hinted at as the cause of her death.

The opportunity came on a day that Cecile had gone to the next village to visit her family. We were at last on our own for more than a few moments. My aunt had been rather peeved that after having spent the last year and a half sending me money and parcels of clothes, I had returned to her with so little. I explained about the money, in more detail than I had been able to do in the letter I had sent her from France. I also told her how Justine would rifle through the parcels addressed to me, and take for herself anything she could use. I also tried to not only explain the family's poverty, but also the scarcity of goods in the shops. However, living in prosperous Switzerland, she could not understand. Three years after the end of the war, France had still not recovered from the destruction caused by the conflict. She then asked why I could not have asked for papa's support to protect my interests, when it came to the content of the parcels. She had by then accepted that I had been powerless when it came to salvaging some of the cash she had sent.

I tried to explain about papa's resentment towards me since he had returned from the war. This was new territory for her, as on my previous visit I had never even hinted that there was a problem between us. I had still felt bound to keep the promise of silence made to my mother. At last this was the moment to put my heavy burden down. So I tried to explain to my aunt, my mother's behaviour with the army of Occupation, as well as the true nature of the illness that had killed her. I had hardly uttered a few sentences, when my aunt exploded in a fury. How dare I talk about my mother in this dreadful way; she never wanted to hear another lie from me. I was to promise never to sell this tissue of fiction to anyone. She was particularly anxious to know if I had so much as hinted to the Miller that my mother had been less than perfect. I reassured her on this point. Anna taught me word for word the story I should tell people who inquired about my experiences during the war. This went from the sainthood of my mother, to never mentioning the word orphanage ever again. I was always to refer to my stay with the nuns as being in boarding school. Any failure to keep strictly to this script would result in the short run to my being sent back to France. In the long run, I would forever be a social outcast. I was very frightened, and promised anything she asked. But the fear of slipping up never left me. The distance that had separated me from people, since my mother extracted a promise of silence from me, grew and grew. I developed a technique for keeping everyone at arm's length for safety. I repeated my aunt's lesson for years, until I almost believed it to be the truth myself.

My aunt was busy getting her stepson's clothes, ready for the start of the school year. So when I mentioned that I was looking forward to the new term, my aunt said casually that it would be useless for me to go to classes. I was to have my sixteenth birthday during the Christmas holidays, and it would be legal for me to start work in the new year. I tried to insist, but her view was that it was useless to educate girls beyond the age of 16. Marriage and children were the future career for girls. It was more important for me to learn to run a house and look after babies. Without any kind of dowry or inheritance to look forward to, it would be hard enough to find me a good husband. In any case, not being a Swiss national, I would not be allowed grants or bursaries for further studies, and free education stopped at sixteen. Of course, it would be different if Maman had not married a Frenchman, who declared me to be his daughter. She would have remained an unmarried mother, and I would be Swiss. I could then have had financial help from the state as an orphan. But what would be the point? Educating girls was a waste of time. That was the end of the discussion.

I was devastated. I had returned from France believing my aunt had given the undertaking that my future would be taken care of. Even my parents had understood it to mean I would be returning to school. In the evening, I shared my distressing news with Louisa and Jacques. Both agreed that my aunt probably had in mind, either a job at one of the mills or domestic work. The family had contacts at both the blanket mill and the fine cloth mill. The former would be out of the question because the sacking of Janot was too recent. The latter was too far from the village. Also in the equation, was the comment from my aunt about the need for me to learn to run a house and look after children.

My family refused to acknowledge that for a long part of my time in France, I had held jobs to the satisfaction of my employers. I had never been considered to be useless using my hands. The Swiss still treated me as if I was a total nullity, a round zero. The reason was simple. The criteria exercised was the same as had been used to judge my ability with knitting needles two years ago. I only knew the French way of doing things. In other words, I was using inferior techniques.

Aunt Anna soon put her cards on the table. I was to work in a house. She scoured the countryside, interviewing prospective employers while I stayed at home. Eventually, the long list she had compiled was reduced to two names, one was Louisa's brother's household, and the other an extended family who lived in the centre of the village.

She soon dismissed Suzy's family, on the ground that her sister-in-law was rather mad. She settled on the extended family. I did not meet the people, until the day after my birthday, when I arrived at 7 am to start work. I felt reasonably positive about this decision, as I was to keep my room at the Miller's. My employers would pay the rent, and offered a salary of 30 Swiss francs a month, a pittance even in those days. I found out through Louisa's sister-in-law what my aunt had told her. In consideration of the fact that I knew nothing, any wages offered would be acceptable. So it was probably what she had said to my future employers. Because I did not live at my place of employment, I felt that I would soon find some other way to plan my future. I may have to be patient, but I would get out of this drudgery.

The house was modern, and exuded comfort and solidity, as did the occupants. The elderly couple shared the house with their married daughter. Mr Moran, the grandfather, still had a hand in running their fuel and transport business, but mostly concentrated on his work as Justice of the Peace. Mme Moran was never idle. She did the weekly washing, she cooked, she mended, and she knitted. Also, bliss of bliss for me, often in the afternoon and the evening she read books. The glass fronted bookcase offered its treasure in the drawing room, so this was a house where reading was not considered a hopeless depravation.

The daughter, Mme Peterson was a quiet young woman in her mid-thirties. Her first child had not yet walked. She shared the domestic chores with her mother, in what seemed to be a perfectly well coordinated duet. She also did all the administrative work for the firm. Her husband Helmut, run the transport business with the help and counsel of his father-in-law.

The general atmosphere of the house was one of harmony. In all the time I worked for the family, I never heard them raise their voices to each other. They all seemed to fit with each other, like a well-designed puzzle.

Their attitude towards me was equally courteous. The women taught me their ways of doing things, and it was not always easy. Ironing was a recurrent bugbear. I had never had to iron tea towels, and fold them in a particular way before. As for men's shirts, I got the hang of the ironing easily enough, but the folding of them had me sweating and trembling.

My job was to do all the rougher work. I was to assist both women in whatever task they were engaged in. So I could, at one moment, be scrubbing two flights of concrete steps, and at the next, be learning to lay the table for a dinner party. I also helped with the care of the baby, when her mother was busy in the office. I ate with the family, unless there were guests. On these occasions I had to have my meal in the kitchen, on the corner of the messy table. This was reminiscent of my meals at the de… in France and I usually ate very little. The exclusion made me feel rather gloomy, and it showed. Mme Moran did not seem to notice, but her daughter did. She thought I was sulking, and teased me gently about it.

The greatest joy of the day was going home to the Miller's every evening. My aunt had asked me to call in to say goodnight on the way to my lodgings. I had to make a long detour to get to her house. I decided that I would soon find a way of getting rid of this unwelcome practice.

Chapter Ten

Towards the end of January, Louisa had almost decided how she
was going to spend Jacques' generous Christmas present. She went to
Lausanne to make a final choice. Would it be a fur coat or a rug for
her sitting room? She came back having bought a beautiful rug, and
would have been happy had she felt well. On that cold Thursday in
January, she had caught a chill. When I arrived at the house that
evening, she was already in bed feeling a little feverish. She assured
me that there was nothing to worry about. But when I returned from
work the following evening, Louisa was quite unwell. She said she
had the flu and that it was normal with this virus to have a high
temperature. When I left for work the next morning, Jacques was still
in their bedroom. I slipped out quietly, as had been the routine since
I had started work. Throughout the day, I became increasingly
anxious. When I took The Petersons' baby, Jenny, for her daily dose
of fresh air, I wandered near Louisa's house. I was hoping to see
someone to whom I could ask how she was.

That evening I did not go to see my family, but went straight from
work to see Louisa. I dismissed as unimportant my aunt's probable
anger, compared with the dreadful feeling of apprehension I had lived
with throughout the day.

As soon as I walked in the house, I knew something was seriously
wrong. Little Lynette had been taken to sleep at a relative's house in
the village. Mad auntie Lizzie was there, looking after Louisa whose
condition had deteriorated throughout the day. On top of the high
fever she now had a violent backache. The doctor had diagnosed

severe influenza and lumbago. When I sat on her bed, she said in an unusually sharp tone, "Be careful, you are causing a draught". Turning towards her sister-in-law, she added that her feet were cold. Lizzie offered to make a hot water bottle. She returned a few moments later, and was about to lift the blanket at the foot of the bed. At that instant, as Louisa's face turned towards me, she had a sudden, massive haemoptysis spray the bed, and both of us, with blood. I called out to her sister-in-law, who shouted to Jacques to fetch the Doctor. Then turning to Louisa she said. "Do not worry, we will clean this up". I said, "She is dead". "No, replied Lizzie. She has fainted". I repeated quietly, "Louisa is dead". Her sister-in-law looked at her closely, and did not say another word.

Despite knowing in my head that Louisa had died, I was still hoping that Dr. Leblanc would prove me wrong. He came in with Jacques and the district nurse. He briefly examined the young woman, who had been joking with him a few hours earlier, and pronounced her dead. Hearing my worst fear confirmed, I started to howl. Jacques held me close to him. I could not stop howling. When at last I regained control of myself, I became aware that the house was full of people. Suddenly the spectre of my aunt's face appeared. I panicked about having lost control in front of people. I made the unforgivable mistake of asking all people present not to tell my aunt of my extreme distress. I feared that she would be angry.

Louisa's family was aware of Aunt Anna's jealousy, and reassured me. However, the district nurse was appalled at the thought that someone could be angry with me at such a time. I was sixteen years old, and had just witnessed someone I loved die. She wanted to know what sort of person could show anger at my distress. At the first opportunity she went to see my aunt. She remonstrated with her. She adorned her story with added details that no one present could ever confirm.

My aunt was very angry. When she came to the house to pay the visit of condolences, I hid. She did not see me until Louisa's funeral. On coming out of the church, my family kidnapped me. My aunt was holding one of my arms, and Janot's wife the other. I was frogmarched to their house, where a dreadful scene took place. When she was safely away from outsiders' ears, Aunt Anna exploded. She gave vent to all the bottled up rage provoked by my entanglement with the Miller's, my callous lack of gratitude, and the public humiliation I had exposed her to with my wild accusations.

I tried to deny some of the things the district nurse had told her. It was not even the kind of language I would use. Until that moment, I may not have had much affection for my aunt, but I had held her in a certain respect. I could even understand her frustration. After this scene, any shred of regard I had for her was lost forever. She insisted I went on my knees and asked her for forgiveness. Under the threat of being sent back to France by the next train, I did as asked. All the while swearing inside my head that I would never go on my knees for anyone ever again.

My aunt informed me that the whole family was very angry with me. Anna said that my grandmother would give me a serious thrashing on my next visit. She insisted that I write a letter to everyone who was at the Miller's house the evening Louisa had died. I was to apologise for having told lies about my aunt. I was forced to say how grateful I was to her for rescuing me from a miserable life in France. She posted the letters herself not trusting me to do so. Most of the people who received a letter had been absorbed in their own grief. They could not make out what this was all about. All but one person ignored it. Dr. Leblanc went to see my aunt, and remonstrated severely with her. He told Jacques that he had said to Anna, "You have given good things to this child with one hand, and taken them away with the other". She was never to forgive him.

Aunt Anna told me that she would make sure the whole village knew of my perversity. No one would ever again be taken in by my beautiful smile and my charm. This statement had the effect of changing not only how I saw myself, but also to warp for ever, my interpretation of the world around me. From that fateful moment, the firm conviction that no one would ever love me, or even like me, grew in me. I started to walk about the village with my head bowed, staring at my feet. I avoided greeting people, and only felt at ease with my own peer group, who were indifferent to my aunt's temper.

Jacques had the interest of little Lynette at heart. He put his resentment aside, and went to see my aunt. He asked her if it would

be possible for me to give up my job at the Moran's, and stay at the
house to take care of the child. I would help his elderly mother, who
had agreed to come in daily. My aunt refused on the ground that it
would not be proper for a girl of 16 to stay in a house with a man who
had no wife. Tortuous negotiations between the Morans, my aunt and
Jacques took place, Dr. Leblanc acting as the honest broker. The adult
world agreed that I could stay to look after Lynette for 4 weeks. After
this time, I must return to the Moran's. The price extracted by my
aunt for consenting to this compromise was that I ought to be lodged
by the Morans, at the end of the month. They generously agreed,
despite the undoubted inconvenience giving me a room would cause
them.

Jacques' mother was very elderly, very short and extremely obese.
She could not pick up anything off the floor, or reach the upper shelf
of the cupboards. In her home, her husband was always at hand, and
now my presence was a help to her. After some initial suspicion on
both sides, we relaxed and formed an odd but efficient team. She was
a superb cook, and a humorous woman. If it had not been for my
profound sadness, our time together could have been riotous.

Lynette had not really taken in what death meant. She had been
told that Louisa had gone to heaven, to be with her little brother
Max. She seemed to think she would be back soon. The little girl was
4 years old, and no-one undertook to make her understand that her
mummy was gone forever. We all had our own grief to cope with. It
suited everybody to keep the child in ignorance of the dreadful finality
of death. It was hard enough to avoid crying in front of her. Once she
had caught me in tears, and I had told her I was missing her mummy.
Putting her arms round my neck, she told me not to be sad, her
mummy would be back soon. I confessed the incident to Jacques, who
was very understanding. However, he said that explaining the reality
of death to Lynette would be more than he felt able to cope with at
that time.

Chapter Eleven

When I returned to the Morans, it was under a very different regime from the one I had enjoyed previously. Being resident, I now felt very much domestic again, and very lonely. I cried a great deal when I thought I was alone. I enjoyed the luxury of a most comfortable room, and the beauty of a superb alpine view. In my free time, I was allowed to read books, which were deemed suitable for a girl my age. They were usually sentimental novels, nothing too raunchy or violent. I could also listen to radio plays with grandmother Moran, and was given a fair amount of time off. But I no longer felt free. I had to be in bed by nine o'clock in the week, and ten on Saturday. All I wanted to do was read until I felt sleepy. But at the appointed hour, Madame Moran would tell me to turn my light off. The first few months, I lay in the dark, sobbing my heart out.

When Easter came, my aunt's stepson had his confirmation. For a Swiss Protestant boy, it was the passport into adulthood. The religious ceremony was to take place in the temple, exactly opposite the Moran's house. I was given elegant clothes and shoes, cast offs of Madame Peterson, so I could be smart for the occasion. I really had no wish to go to a family celebration. Madame Moran had thought a festive day with the family might improve the relationships. In any event, I was not invited. I watched from the kitchen window, as a large contingent of my family arrived at the temple.

During the month I had spent looking after Lynette, I had only visited my aunt when summoned. Every visit ended in a row. Once she put her arm up preparing to hit me, I said to her, "if you hit me, I will hit you back". She looked at me in shocked disbelief, but lowered her arm. When I went back to work, I never once visited members of the family, unless I was ordered to do so. Six months later, on one such a visit to Aunt Anna, she told me that my grandmother had complained that she never saw me. I replied tartly that I would have been very stupid to visit someone who had promised me a thrashing. My aunt replied, "Oh! But that was in the past". Their past, perhaps. Not mine.

When I went to the mill, my grandmother was rather apologetic about her previous outburst. She said it was a pity that the family had not known that the nurse was a dreadful gossip, given to confabulations. She told me that she had also blamed Anna for giving credence to the woman without hearing me out. Aunt Theresa was her usual indifferent self, but she was not hostile. I did not warm to my grandmother, and I took Theresa's indifference as I always had done, philosophically.

I would now be able to pay the occasional visit to the mill without being coerced. It was more than I could ever achieve with Aunt Anna, for whom I now had a profound, enduring loathing.

The only family reunion I ever attended after that was a dinner held at the mill. My grandmother had bought and engraved with their initials signet rings for all her grandsons. She gave the rings to the boys, ending up her distribution by declaring in a very satisfied voice. "Now, all my grandchildren have a souvenir of me". Several pairs of eyes turned towards me, but it was young Claude who said, "not all of us. Clara has not been given a ring". At this point my grandmother left the room. She came back a few moments later holding a beautiful ring set with a ruby, the likes of which I was never to see again. I accepted the ring gracefully, but I was even more embarrassed at owning it than my grandmother had been at being coerced into giving it to me. I promptly lost it.

The Morans treated me with benevolent condescension. Madame Peterson gave me quality, even elegant clothes and shoes, which she had discarded. I was not quite as frumpish as I had been wearing my middle age aunt's cast offs. I was now living out of an elegant second hand wardrobe that was still too old for me.

My employers expected a fair amount of work from me, but respected my need for free time. They wished I did not spend it mostly closeted in my room reading. After a few months, they virtually threw me out of the house on my afternoons and evenings off. They forced me to attend village fetes, and gave me a full gymnastic kit so I could join the athletic club. Dr. Leblanc had said I should get out of the corset I had worn for years to support my weak back, and do exercises instead. The reason for refusing to join the club had been that I could not afford to buy the kit. My poverty became the welcome accomplice to my loathing of sports. My family's advice for curing my back was that I should always go to bed early. I hated that, at least as much as I hated gymnastics. The class always ended with a game of netball. I was so bad at it that I could never remember which team I was on. I just ran backward and forward across the court in an aimless pursuit of the ball. Most of the other girls soon took a violent dislike to me. I was responsible for the club loosing most matches, as well as all the competitions. But I was only there for my back. Some people were witty enough to applaud me when I arrived minutes after the other runners competing on the 100 meters run. They pretended that I had won the next race. After a national competition, the club came back without a single team medal. My friend Angela told me that I was going to be asked to leave. So I announced loudly that I was resigning. I spoke the truth when I said I was finding the whole thing boring.

Madame Moran was aware that I had some ambition, and would like to leave my servant status behind. But the economic realities of my situation were only too apparent. She thought I was very good with the babies, and suggested that I trained as a nanny. Most courses were very expensive, so out of my league. There was a course run by a Catholic order, which was free for Catholic girls. Despite the detestation I had for nuns, I agreed to the scheme. It seemed the only way I could see of getting out of my hopeless situation. I would, of course, have no income during the two years the course lasted. It was expected that I should give some service to the nursery at the end of the training. So some serious savings would have to be made before I could even consider applying. It was certainly impossible for me to save much on my tiny income. After nearly two years at the Morans, I decided to apply for a job at one of the mills. The choice of the factory would have to be made, taking into account family configurations. I would have preferred to go to the blanket mill, which was near the village, and close to what little social life I was able to enjoy. But it was very near Aunt Anna's house, unfortunately. It would be a daily stress trying to avoid her interferences. The tweed mill was further away. It would mean a move to the next village, but it was a more practical solution. However, in the end, my choice was dictated by an unexpected emotional earthquake.

Chapter Twelve

I still paid regular visits to Suzy's grave, in the evenings when there was no-one about. On one such visit, I accidentally met Jacques just as he was leaving the cemetery. We still shared a very affectionate relationship, and he gave me his usual fatherly hug. But I could not get out of his arms. We started to hold each other too close for a parental greeting. A violent storm gathered up inside me, just as I saw the spectre of my aunt rising between us. We pulled away from each other sharply. Jacques was the one to speak, saying, "I would never want to do you any harm". I let him go, cursing my cowardice and his decency. That moment changed our relationship; we were now very careful with each other. A few months later, he had a fling with a local waitress. She soon declared him to be the father of her unborn child, and he married her. I was almost 18 and he was nearly 38 years old. On talking confidentially about my legal situation with Judge Moran, I found out too late that my aunt had no authority over me for two reasons. She had never been made my legal guardian, and my nationality. Being French I would have been allowed to marry at 15 years and 3 months, and not at 20, as Swiss law demanded. When special conditions such as a pregnancy occurred, permission to wed could be granted to Swiss youngsters before the legal age.

Knowing that my aunt had no power over me, fed my anger and resentment towards her. I had allowed myself to be blackmailed into submission. This was because I had not known that the moment I was financially independent from her, she could do me no harm. The family had refused to buy me the Swiss nationality on my first visit to Switzerland, the reason being that a previous generation of relatives had gone back to their country of origin, Germany. This was after a considerable sum of money had been spent making them Swiss citizens. Even on my first stay in the country, the leitmotiv had been, marry a Swiss and you will be Swiss at no cost at all. I felt that I did not belong to this family, nor did I have any allegiance to the country. The moment I started work, my passport was in the custody of the Police des Etrangers. It was to them that I had to report any change of address, employment, or civil status. Not to the family.

Working at a factory was the start for me of a dislocated existence. I rented a room at Aunt Theresa's married son Eric's house, and had my meals at the mill, a mile away. The week I was on the early morning shift, I had to walk the extra mile on the way to the factory to pick up the food my aunt had prepared for me the evening before. She did this last thing at night, so the content of the thermos was still lukewarm. My cousin's Swiss-German wife Erica, refused to allow me to prepare a hot drink on her stove. She maintained that my fiddling in her kitchen would interfere with their own breakfast, when we all worked on the same shift. The noise I would be making in the kitchen would wake them up early when they were on a late turn. I paid the going rate for the renting of the room, and the catering my aunt provided for me. I shared no social life in either of the houses. I was not really welcome at my cousin's abode. At the mill, I lacked patience with young Claude, and my grandmother's endless fussing over him.

While remaining on good terms with my Catholic friends, I spent less time with them. I became closer to Angela whom I had known since attending school on my previous visit. She was a budding poet, who kept her literary activities secret from her market gardening family. We shared a love of writing. Angela enjoyed sitting in a local bar, playing the jukebox and having a few drinks. I joined her there when I could. The two of us exchanged confidences, talking about our hopes of a writing future. We chained smoked, and listened to the tune of 'The Third Man' repeatedly. Being forced to listen to the same music for hours, we drove the other customers into a paroxysm of fury. Angela could get merry on very few drinks, but I never got drunk, no matter how many glasses of wine I imbibed. I had trained my head to be immune to the effects of alcohol. I was too aware that getting even a little tipsy would be very dangerous for me. I had too many secrets to keep, and could not allow myself the pleasure of this kind of relaxation. The only effect alcohol had on me was to make my deepest sadness come dangerously near the surface. On many evenings we just drank coffee. Towards the end of the week when money was running out, we made a cup last until the bar owner started giving us odd looks. I smoked heavily, and in public, at a time when in rural Switzerland, women were not seen smoking.

Aunt Anna inevitably found out about my smoking. She summoned me to her house, and made a full on scene reproaching me my way of life, and threatening me with dire consequences. Knowing that she had no real power over me, I answered in a most insolent manner, even laughing in her face. I yelled at her that I wanted to be free. This cry became the refrain, I intoned on every occasion I was called to order. This was the last time she raised her arm to hit me. As I had on the first occasion I said to her, "If you hit me I will hit you back". She did not touch me.

My hatred of her had increased since my talk with Judge Moran. I blamed her for the fear she had sowed in me, which had prevented me from exploring further my relationship with Jacques. I had met him once when I was on a walk with Angela. We greeted each other too carefully, my casual greeting hiding I hoped, the violent need I had of throwing myself in his arms. When he had walked away, Angela said, "What is it between the two of you?" She would not take my "nothing" for an answer. "Well", she said, "I know what I saw, and that was two magnets trying too hard not to touch each other". I explained to her what had happened in the cemetery, and her fury with my aunt was almost equal to mine. Because of Jacques' resemblance to the French couturier Pierre Balmain, this is how he was henceforth referred to between us. There was relief, as well as sadness, in my being able to share this secret with my only trusted friend.

About this time the whole family began to put pressure on me to get married. I was expected to wed a young man of their choice. Nicholas was not a local boy, but a Swiss-German, who had come to work in a flourmill in a nearby village. He soon made an impression on everyone, with his prowess at the gymnasium. Despite his puny physique, he was an accomplished athlete. But when he walked, he had a way of swinging his backside, which was not very masculine. This would have put me off him, even if I had not been dead set against the match. The most upsetting aspect of the situation was the fact that my cousins put even more pressure on me than the older generation did. It was partially a question of "Gros Sous" as Nicholas's parents were mill owners. But it was the family's hope to have me off its back forever, which prompted this harassment.

I was never short of suitors though. There was always someone offering to take me home after a dance. In the winter, one could be out dancing most weekends, and starting the night with Angela, I usually did. We were very popular with the young men, and rarely danced with the same one twice. Angela was very pretty, and she knew all the local lads, which was a good launching pad for the evening. I thought I was rather plain, and my popularity surprised me. The young men who offered to take me home willingly walked a couple of kilometres to my door. There, if I liked the lad, we shared a single passionate goodnight kiss, then I left him breathless on the doorstep. No one got any more than that, or even demanded it. If I felt a rise of the phoenix, I pretended I had not noticed. I curtailed the kiss, and dived in the house.

My favourite escort was an older man; an Italian gardener who worked for Angela's family. Alberto gave me a fatherly kiss on the cheek, and waited until I had opened the door. Then he walked back to the village, sometimes through rain or snow. I never felt unhappy after coming home with Alberto.

When I was escorted by one of the lads, once in the safety of my room, I often threw myself fully clothed on the bed in sobs. Only to repeat the experience the following weekend.

I was very unhappy staying at my cousin's house. Eric, my aunt's son, was a mild mannered fellow. But his wife, whom my grandmother insisted on referring to as "l'allemande" was a hard and mean woman. She would not allow me to use the lavatory at night, in case I made noise and woke her up; so she supplied me with a chamber pot. I was so humiliated that I waited until the couple were out of the house to empty it. This sometimes took a couple of days. I did not keep the room tidy, and it soon became rather sordid.

When Christmas came "l'allemande" asked me if I could help her get ready for the feast. Thinking it might improve her attitude towards me, I willingly agreed. I worked hard all day, cleaning, polishing and cooking. We had a brief pause at lunchtime when she gave me a mug of tea, a slice of bread and a gendarme, a thin, dried sausage. After which we resumed the preparations for Christmas.

When all was done, I was hungry and exhausted. I told "l'allemande" that I was tired. "Well, she said, I am not stopping you from going to bed".

I had been lying down a few minutes, when the smell of cooking pervaded my room. The aroma of fried food was a torture to my starving stomach and I cried.

Soon after that I discovered that "l'allemande" was taking her friends on a tour of my room when I was out. She had to prove to them what a slut I was. That was the last straw, and I decided to leave.

Chapter Thirteen

Angela's parents agreed to give me temporary shelter, in a comfortable room with access to decent sanitation. I was dreading telling my grandmother that I was leaving my cousin's house. I told Claude who explained the reasons to her. For once, she was on my side and agreed that "l'allemande" had just been too mean. Food was very important in my mother's family. Both my mother and Aunt Anna were superb cooks. My grandmother and Aunt Elisa may not have been quite so fine, but there was always plenty of robust, appetizing food on the table at the mill.

I now had to add nearly two kilometres to my walk to work. In the winter it meant struggling through the overnight fall of snow, when I was on the morning shift. But the bliss of being away from the Nazi monster made it worthwhile.

A Swiss-German girl I had met at the youth club invited me to visit Zurich during the Carnival. I took the few days leave I was due, and went home with Ruthie.

While I was away, my aunt received a form from the Catholic nursery, to which I had applied for training as a nursery nurse. This demanded that she gave her consent to my undertaking the course of study. She replied to the nuns that she could do no such thing. She felt in her conscience that I was a most unsuitable person to undertake such a course. As an example, she gave my debauched behaviour as demonstrated by the fact that I had gone to the Carnival. There, it was obvious, I would be drinking, dancing and doing god only knew what else. On my return from Zurich, she made a point of telling me what she had done. I soon received a letter telling me that I had indeed been refused a place on the course.

Enduring the awful drudgery of working at the factory, and saving what money I could, had become pointless. I also had to send endless parcels, and what money I could afford to satisfy the demands of my stepmother. So I had not really enjoyed the extra earnings, work at the factory afforded me. I decided to leave the village and go to Lausanne. There, I hoped I could at least pursue my education by working in the day, and attending evening classes.

When I was seventeen, I had gone to the French Consulate to ask for advice. I hoped to be helped to find a solution to my predicament. I told the person who saw me that my family had refused to let me pursue my studies. The woman took less than a minute to grab me by the shoulder, and pushed me out of the building. All she said was, "your family brought you here, let them help you".

It was a very hot day. I had such a bad headache that I could hardly see when I found myself on the pavement outside the Consulate. I was sobbing, several people passed by, all ignored me. Many Swiss people are like that. When I had calmed down, I realised that I was alone in the world. But I must never expose myself to such humiliation again. The experience had been horrible. It became both a source of strength and alienation for me. When I had recovered, a voice in my head said, "you are on your own, on your own, mate". What the echo sent back was. "Never allow anyone to get so close, that you become dependent and forget this truth". I set about looking for a job in town, which would allow me to earn my living, and leave me time to attend classes. I was so disorientated by then that I did not know any more what I wanted to learn. Having been prevented from pursuing the course of studies in the subjects, which had been my passion, I no longer knew which way to go. I had it all worked out when I was 14 years old. I wanted to study literature, and law, so as to have something solid to fall back on until I became a successful writer. Now, at nearly twenty, I plunged almost blindly into the future. I thought vaguely I should do a German course. I knew that in Switzerland, without languages I had no hope of improving my lot. I was totally unfocused, but I felt that if I went on learning I would get somewhere in the end.

Being without a diploma, or even a certificate of apprenticeship proved a serious handicap in trying to find a non-residential job. In a country where even shop assistants, and most hotel staff had to serve an apprenticeship, the only unskilled jobs available to me would not keep a roof over my head. I had to accept that a residential job was my only hope to get out both of the factory and the family's orbit.

I scanned the newspapers advertisements, and went to a few interviews for unqualified nannies. Pointing to my severe acne, one woman told me that she could not have a girl with a dirty face caring for her children. After a few more failures, I did secure a post in the household of a wealthy industrialist. There I had the total care of four children, whose ages ranged from 6 months to 9 years. The mother's contribution to her children's day was to shout from the landing on the floor below towards the upstairs nursery, "Good morning my darlings". Then she was off to the yacht club most days. She usually returned at lunchtime, berated the maid, the washer woman and the lady who came weekly to do the ironing. The turnover of staff was such that in the seven months I lived with this family, we went through three maids, 3 washer women and at least an equal number of ironing ladies. The instability of the household induced in me the fear of dismissal, which because of my rootless existence, was terrifying. Every time Madame was in a bad mood, I was sure to be dismissed. She declared herself more than happy with my care of the baby and the sweet Axel, who was three years old. However, she became increasingly critical of my handling of the two elder children. The nine-year-old girl, whom I was supposed to help with her homework, was already studying poetry and Greek mythology. While I was at home with Ronsart, and had the luck of knowing by heart the pieces she was studying, I was totally at sea with the Greek gods. Elisabeth was also very scathing of my clothes, and the odd Vaudois expressions I had picked up over the years.

The care of the seven-year-old boy Gregoire had me in a constant state of anxiety. He was an unhappy nervy child, who masturbated constantly. I was unable to cope with it, and with him. When I tried to discuss the child's problems with his mother, she put the onus on me, berating me for my lack of psychology.

I had some evenings off in the week. I joined a German class, although I was so tired at the end of the day that I fell asleep during the lesson, on occasions. Most of the students were foreigners, and showed me much kindness. One young Portuguese man often took me home on his scooter. I sometimes dozed on his back during the short journey.

I formed a bond with the third maid who came to the house, a witty, educated Austrian girl, who had come to Switzerland to perfect her French. But the jolly Heidi, who had arrived from Gras, was transformed in a few weeks into sobbing misery by the endless harassing of Madame. In less than 3 months she was gone.

I too was on my way out. I had become so tense and exhausted that my shredded nerves could not handle the situation. I was expecting the sack every time Madame's mood unnerved me. To avoid being dismissed I left.

The next few jobs ended in ever shortening periods. Every time my employer looked disgruntled, I took it personally and gave notice before I was dismissed. At night I laid in bed, mentally packing and unpacking my suitcases at an ever increasing rate. The spiral was going downward, and the rings were getting smaller at a speed, which could only end in disaster. I was lucid enough to ask myself what would happen when the rings had shrunken to a dot, but not sufficiently to take it in, when my employers expressed regret that I was leaving them.

The last few jobs were in Yverdon. I had by then renounced the idea of looking after children. I worked in a bakery where the boss was very easy going, but invariably forgot to pay my wages. When I reminded her, all she would say was "just go and buy what you need and bring me the bills". When I tried to insist on being paid my agreed dues, for the first time she looked peeved. I felt I had made a mistake. I began to feel insecure, and fearing the sack I looked for another job.

I soon found a position in a patisserie, a few hundred yards away. It was a big establishment. The family's living quarters were above the shop, as was the accommodation of the residential staff. I shared a room with the "cook general". The apprentices were lodged in the rafters, and of my job was to wake them up after their afternoon sleep. The rest of the time I was to help wherever I was needed. The boss lady seemed to take a dislike to me on sight, as I never seemed to be where she wanted me. She seemed to think that I should guess when there was a rush in the shop, and appear there to help her. But tucked away in the kitchen on the floor above, I had no idea what was going on below. Her angry voice called me from the bottom of the stairs. I then had to wash my hands, change my apron, and check my general appearance before going downstairs. I had not been accustomed to a very elegant way of boxing the patisserie, while I worked at the family bakery. My clumsiness, added to the nervousness induced by the boss's irritation, made sure that I was not doing anything to her satisfaction.

However, it was the staff's catering which caused me to be dismissed after a week. The breakfast we were served consisted of the usual Swiss menu at the time: bread, butter and jam and a bowl of coffee. The midday meal was invariably some sort of pasta or rice and salad. For the evening meal we were given leftover cakes with *café au lait* and nothing else. Nothing savory ever, just cakes and cakes! I enjoyed one piece of patisserie or even two, but a whole meal of it, evening after evening, no! After a week of this regime, even the thought of eating another cake made me nauseous. I innocently asked the "cook general" if it was possible for me to have a sandwich. She reported to Madame that I had complained about the food. I was summoned to see the lady. It was late in the evening, when she informed me that as I was dissatisfied with the food, she wanted me to leave, and to leave now. Swiss law, apparently allowed both employers and staff to terminate a post any time during the first ten days of employment, without further formalities. I pointed out to the woman that I was an orphan, and had no home to go to. Her curt reply was, "that is not my affair; I am not sentimental". She eventually agreed to let me stay until the 10th day, when I would indeed be gone.

Chapter Fourteen

Luckily for me, I was not socially isolated in Yverdon as I had been in Lausanne. I had already made friends. I dashed to their house more as a need to talk about my plight, than expecting practical help from them. However, my friend's father played cards every weekend in a large café in the centre of the town. He remembered having heard the owner complaining about the shortage of staff. The next day I was engaged, again as a general helper. The salary was better than I had earned in all my previous residential posts. There was also the certainty of getting tips, when I helped in the café. I was to share a bedroom with the young Italian widow Lisa, who worked in the kitchen.

While in Lausanne, I had begun to think that living in Switzerland much longer would result in driving me mad, or killing me. I did not blame the country, not yet. How could one blame it, was it not perfect? It obviously was my fault, if I failed to meet the exacting standards expected in this land of paragons. I had realized by then that the French motto of Liberty, Egality, Fraternity had in Switzerland been replaced by Money, Work and Cleanliness. There was no room for human frailty; if you were not perfect by Helvetic standards, you may as well be annihilated. The Swiss kept giving Henry Dunant, as an example of their altruism and humanity. But the founder of the Red Cross was definitely the swallow that did not make a summer.

I began to make plans about leaving the country as soon as I reached my French majority. I had to avoid at all costs, my parents becoming involved in my life. I could not risk Aunt Anna contacting them during my minority. That gave me almost half a year to economise enough to pay my fare to Canada, where I hoped to go. While on a long train journey, I had got into a conversation with a French Canadian family. They had told me a lot about their country, including the fact that it was bilingual. Living there would give me the chance to learn English, which until then had seemed an impossible ambition to achieve. They told me about educational opportunities, which were not closed to foreigners in their country as they were in Switzerland. The family gave me their visiting card. They offered me their hospitality, a few Canadians coins and some "jetons" in case I needed them for the phone when I arrived.

I was now able to look forward more optimistically to the future. I had at last the hope of escaping the straight jacket, in which I had felt paralysed for nearly five years. I relaxed, and was able to enjoy some harmless flirtations. One of these, however, went somewhat further than my usual doorstop kiss. Bertrand, the son of the Pinnard, came back from the sanatorium in Leysin where he had been treated for tuberculosis. He had, apparently, become infected while doing his military service. He was a handsome young man, very seductive. He pursued me relentlessly. I allowed myself to believe him, when he declared having fallen desperately in love with me. We kissed in the wine cellar, behind the bar and anywhere we could get a few instants of privacy. I permitted him the kind of liberties I had never indulged in before.

One night Lisa forgot to lock our bedroom door. Bertrand let himself in, and climbed in bed with me. I kept repeating, "Lisa, Lisa", to which he answered, "She is asleep". Although the activities went rather further than it had been possible in corners downstairs, I would not give him what he really wanted. He left saying he loved me more than ever, and teasingly added that I deserved a certificate proving my virginity. The following nights he came and shook the door until I opened it. Telling myself that more noise would wake up Lisa, I let him in. I never gave him all he longed for, but he returned every night until he had to rejoin his regiment. He wrote me a few love letters, the last one telling me he would soon be home on leave, then silence.

When he came back he was accompanied by a rather tarty girl, who stayed in his room. He hadn't said a word to me, apart from the barest civil greetings. I was rather surprised that I was not really upset. But so glad I was that I had not given my all to him. I then knew that I did not love him. I had enjoyed the experience, and learned a lot from it. The rest would have to wait.

When I talked about it with Lisa, she assured me that no one downstairs had been aware of Bertrand's nightly visits. She was surprised to hear that we had been kissing in corners for weeks. She owned up to have been wide awake when he visited me at night. She told me so with a giggle. She had obviously enjoyed the spectacle. She also said to me that on each of his previous leaves from the army, Bertrand had come home with a whore, who almost never left his room. Apparently he never appeared with the same girl twice. Rather shocked by her use of the term whore, I asked if it was how she saw me. "Oh! No", she said, "I thought he had fallen in love, as you were so different from these girls".

Soon after this conversation, I got up one morning to find that Lisa had done a midnight flit. Her cupboard and drawers were empty, and so was one of my mother's earrings from which she had squeezed the stones, perhaps testing their potential as diamonds. She had left me the empty shell and taken the intact earring away. Her escape must have been planned, as she would have had to show the receipt from the tax office before she could retrieve her passport from the Police des Etrangers. This left me without the only memento I had of my mother. It was a poor consolation, that I now had the sole enjoyment of this large room, the next maid not needing to be resident.

Chapter Fifteen

Madame Pinnard had gone away for the weekend, leaving her husband in charge of the café. Mr Pinnard was a purple-faced, boozy man in his fifties, who suffered from chronic bronchitis. Unlike his still dashing wife, he was a rather unattractive fellow. He normally spent his time going from table to table playing cards and drinking red wine with the customers. He never interfered with the running of the café, and only addressed the staff to order more wine. We did not take much notice of him.

The weekend his wife was away the waitress did all the organising. She asked one of the part-time workers to come in to work in the kitchen. She wanted me to be free to help her in the bar. As was usual at the end of the week, more men came to play cards and the red wine flowed freely. After each game, the loser bought a fresh bottle. The Sunday customers were the local bankers, businessmen and well to do pensioners. They were very generous tippers. The waitress allowed me a fair share of the bonanza.

At the end of the day, being very tired, I retired to my room early. I was about to get into bed, when there was a knock at the door. Thinking it could only be Mr Pinnard, I felt safe. I opened the door, and asked him what he wanted. It was simple enough, he said there were only the two of us in the house and what he wanted was me. As he said this he tried to grab me, but I fled from him. There followed a pursuit around the room, in which I tried hard not to be cornered. I instinctively knew, that if this happened I would be lost. At first he thought I was just playing hard to get, and he was laughing. But when he realised I was in earnest, he became very angry. Mercifully, I had youth and agility on my side, and he had age and bad health against him. Eventually, I got near the window, which I opened, threatening to jump if he did not leave at once. The police station was immediately opposite the café, on the other side of the narrow street. Even in his half-drunken state, it must have occurred to him that it would be hard to explain why a twenty year old girl, who was laughing and joking in the café less than an hour earlier, suddenly landed on the steps of the police station. He ran out of the room.

I locked the door, and pushed a bed against it for added security. I was very shaken, but I knew too well what the Swiss's attitude was towards foreigners. There was nowhere I could go to complain about my ordeal. I just had to get out, but how? I spent the night trying out plans of evasions and dismissing one after the other. By morning, I thought I had found an idea worth trying.

Monday was my day off. I did not get out of my room but listened all day until I heard Madame Pinnard's voice. I went downstairs and asked her for three weeks holiday. I said that I wanted to go to France to see my family. As I was not entitled to more than a few days leave, she refused. I gave her my notice to quit. My plan appeared to have worked, and the backfiring when it came was all the more traumatic for it.

I gave up all idea of looking for another job in Switzerland. But the price for a quick exit was the sacrificing of my Canadians' plans. I had not enough funds yet to finance the journey. Another solution was possible. Recently, I had met a young woman who had just returned from spending two years working in an English family. She was very enthusiastic about everything British. I sought her out, and was informed by her that her former bosses who lived in Kent, were again looking for a girl. They had had to get her successor deported because she was out of control. Lilly wrote to the Noble family on my behalf, presenting me as a very desirable candidate for the post of resident domestic. She explained to me that in order to be able to stay in England more than a year it was safer to acquire a working permit. She assured me that the work would be the same as if I was an *au pair*. It would just be an added security, should I wish to stay in

England indefinitely. I expressed to her the urgency of my need, having already given notice at my current post. She booked an international phone call at the post office. After a brief discussion with Mrs Noble, Lilly helped me gather up all the necessary documents, which were sent by express post. All I had to do was wait.

The friends who had helped me secure the job at the café were not too pleased with me. I told them that I was leaving because I had not been able to obtain the amount of leave I had demanded. The father went so far as to say that it was not like me to behave in this unreasonable manner. I was already in a precarious emotional state, and the reproaches were more than I could take. I dissolved into sobs. On promises that my disclosures would not go any further I told him the whole story. He renewed his assurances of discretion. However, the following Sunday after too much wine, and losing a few card games to Mr Pinnard, my friend's father started teasing my boss about the incident of the previous weekend. Madame overheard the remarks, but she did not confront me. Instead she spoke about it to the waitress, with whom she was very close. The girl then told me that I was going to be sued for spreading lies. She said that as I would never have enough money to pay a severe fine and compensation. I was sure to end in jail. Even my assurances that I was telling the truth made no differences to the threats. She assured me that no one was going to take the word of an alien against the declarations of a Swiss citizen.

Madame Pinnard disappeared for several days. The waitress informed me that she had gone all over Switzerland to interview former members of staff. I would be dealt with on her return, according to the results of her inquiries. I was in a state of acute anxiety, and knew that I needed the counsel of a wiser person. I went to see the local Catholic priest, to whom I told the whole story. I was particularly exercised as to what I should answer, if Madame Pinnard questioned me on her return. His advice to me was to tell the lady that she should ask her husband. I could only answer for my own behaviour, not his. After he had said a short prayer, and given me his benediction, I left feeling somewhat relieved.

However, the state of apprehension did not leave me for long. I could not eat or sleep. Every time a policeman came into the café, I shook in case he had come to arrest me. As the café was so close to the police station, it was the obvious meeting place for the officers. I paid my taxes, and armed with my receipt I retrieved my passport from the Police des Etrangers, which calmed me a little.

When Madame Pinnard returned, she went on treating me with the civility she had always shown me. Only the waitress kept on with her menaces. The day I left the café, I avoided Mr Pinnard. On giving me my wages, his wife shook hands with me, and just said, "thank you". Whenever I recalled the episode in the ensuing years, I always wondered what had been the meaning of her thanks.

PART TWO

THE WISENING UP OF THE MONKEY

Chapter Sixteen

I arrived at London's Victoria station with £2 in my pocket. It was all that was left of my savings, after the expenses of the journey. I carried 2 small suitcases of books and clothes. My knowledge of English consisted of three words, and a full sentence I had picked up from a popular song. It was just enough to get me into trouble, but not enough to get me out of it.

But on that first evening, my only concern was to be sure to recognize the gentleman who was going to meet me. I had no photograph of him, only the description given to me by the former *au pair*, Lily. Her vision of the man may be warped by love. He, at least, had the advantage of having a photograph of me. The gentleman found me among the crowd of commuters trying to get on their train home.

The drive to the outskirt of Edenbridge was mostly silent, as Mister David Noble spoke very little French. I was very tired and so overwhelmed by finding myself sitting in his luxury car that I hardly dared breathe. I took in the grimness of the London suburbs. The rows of identical houses, the grey sky and the general gloominess dampened my already fragile spirit. I cheered up somewhat as we got into the Kent countryside, as even in early September it was still a joy to the eyes.

My thoughts were mostly concentrated on speculation as to what my future held. Lily had spoken to me in eulogistic terms of the beautiful mansion I was to live in. Her description of its inhabitants was such that I felt I was entering into the world described in romantic novels.

The mansion was indeed enormous. It made even the large town residence of the de... in Avranches look like a doll's house. The entrance hall itself could have comfortably lodged a large family. The rest of the house was in keeping with this feature.

The grounds were also extensive, and necessitated the employment of a full time gardener. Lilly had told me, that the only other help in the house was a woman who came in most days for a few hours. Mrs Noble cooked the meals, but the rest of the domestic work was to be my responsibility.

Five people lived in the house. Mrs Noble and her husband Adam, their eldest son, who was divorced, Mr David, and his two boys were also permanent residents. The youngest son, Mr Christopher, was a purser in the merchant navy. He appeared only when his ship was in dock.

I was given a pleasant bedroom, but the lovely royal blue bedspread hid two threadbare blankets. The only heating I could look forward to when winter came was fixed to the wall, a two bar electric fire. The rest of the house was heated centrally.

Mrs Noble spoke French fluently, and at first was willing to explain what was expected of me. It was only when things started going wrong that she lost her patience. She often screamed at me that she wished I could speak English. And going wrong they did, very quickly.

The problems, which emerged were two fold. They were those inherent to the upper middle class culture in which I now found myself, with its deeply ingrained snobbery. As important, if not more, were the after effects of the troubled years I had lived in Switzerland, compounded by the dramatic last weeks at the Pinnards.

Mrs Noble or Lizzy, as all the family called her, was closely related to the owners of one of the country's shipping lines. She had been brought up in all the best, and the worst traditions of her class.

She still had in late middle age a more than competent, well trained soprano voice. But singing professionally had been out of the question for her. Her emotional rendering of "The Last Rose of Summer" will be in my ears forever.

The lady told me that she had changed her church, because the vicar had preached that foreigners and coloured people were her equals. The political principles I had been taught by my stepmother, were definitely on the left side of the spectrum. I was shocked by what I saw as a rather fascist attitude.

The dog Tipper hated the postman, and was now under a death sentence after having bitten the man three times. I found Mrs Noble in flood of tears, and inquired as to what was upsetting her. Her answer was "Poor Tipper is having to be put down for the sake of that awful postman". I was later informed that a generous donation had saved the bulldog.

When Mister David accidentally killed an old man on a zebra crossing, the lady told me that it did not really matter, because the victim was "a low class man".

I soon found out why the girl who had replaced Lilly, had been sent back to Switzerland under police escort. She had proved to be out of control, by going to have a drink in the quiet village pub, accompanied by another *au pair* who lived nearby. This last discovery made me extremely nervous, as the last thing I could have coped with was to be packed off anywhere in the world.

My already fragile state was seriously aggravated as a result of my own naivety. Before I left Switzerland, I had given my new address to a part time helper at the Pinnards. She had been the only person to show me a semblance of friendship when the crisis occurred. I had believed her declarations of loyalty and concern. Very soon after my arrival in Kent, I began to receive insulting and threatening letters. It seemed that my former colleague had given my address to whoever asked for it. None of the mail was sent by the Pinnards themselves, all came from members of staff past and present. Every morning, it was my duty to take the mail from the letterbox and sort it out. Most days, I was shaking, and it took me increasingly longer to recover my composure as time went by.

The meals were a torture. There was always very little to eat. The only meal I could satisfy my hunger was breakfast, as Madame was still in bed. The men and the children all had cooked breakfast, and so I benefited from the tradition. Lunch was thin sandwiches, as was tea taken on the dot at 4 o'clock every afternoon. If the men came home we had a cooked meal in the evening. However, if they stayed at their clubs in London, we had soup followed by bread and cheese.

Butter was still rationed in 1953, and Madame allocated herself all the household allocation of this commodity. She had recently had treatment for a gastric ulcer, and margarine was said to be bad for her.

The meals were a source of tension because I found it difficult to learn all the ritual involved, in what is considered good English table manners. About that time, the writer Pierre Daninos wrote in his book, LES CARNETS DU MAJOR THOMPSON, "The   English have taught the world table manners, but it is the French people who eat". I became frightened that I may use the wrong cutlery, or even the right one the wrong way. So I was unable to enjoy the little there was to eat.

I soon discovered that Lilly had been so popular because in the words of Mrs Noble, she was such a hard worker and she ate so little. The implication was that I ate too much. The love affair Lilly had with David was still a secret. I wondered if the delicacies she had told me he brought her from London were more substantial than the sweets and chocolates I had assumed them to be.

Lilly had told me that the romance had been kept a secret because of David's divorce. She was Roman Catholic and was trying to sort out if his registry office first marriage made a difference to the church's attitude. She hoped to clarify the situation with her village priest before the couple could announce their commitment to the Noble family. She had told me that was the reason why she had come home. She could not communicate with the Irish Catholic priest in Edenbridge.

I was feeling very lonely. The children were very self-contained. They did not get much attention from their father, and neither Mr Noble nor his wife seemed to give them a lot of their time. One of my first tasks had been to sew name tabs on a trunk full of school uniforms for the eleven-year-old Nigel. He was soon to become a boarder. The youngest, Luc, who was nine was a very unhappy little boy. He seemed to go around with a handkerchief in his hands, and he often cried. When I first arrived, he was at times quite unkind to me, sniggering at my English pronunciation. However, one day he saw me crying, and after that we had an unspoken understanding. Nothing was ever said by him or me, but he never was unpleasant towards me again. He often gave me little presents, such as a pack of cards or small ornaments.

The boy's mother visited one weekend for the purpose of introducing her fiancé. Luc sat at the table, crying and twisting his handkerchief. Despite my own unhappiness, I wanted to hold the little boy and console him. All the while, his family was telling him that his behaviour was not an acceptable way to treat visitors. Later Mrs Noble told me how the children had come to live in the house. A few years earlier, she had been out for the day with her husband. On their return, they found both children in the garage attached to a fixed point on the wall. Nigel, who was five, was standing by the pushchair in which Luc was tied. The children narrowly escaped being run over by her husband, who did not expect them to be there. Mister David had given up his London house, and joined his children in the parental home.

My position in the house meant that I could do nothing to help the little boy. I was, in any event, getting increasingly fragile. I lost a lot of weight, which I could ill afford after the loss I had already sustained as a result of the Pinnard incident. I kept my skirts up with safety pins, all my other garments felt loose on me. The attacks of panic I had daily when sorting the post, began to occur at other times, in totally unthreatening situations. I had one when I was having a bath, another time I was petrified in the middle of a Woolworth store.

I was allowed out twice a week. On Sunday mornings, I met the *au pair* girl who lived down the road. We both took the bus to Edenbridge to attend mass. I was not allowed to frequent her at other times. Mrs Noble did not consider her a suitable person. The lady blamed her for persuading my predecessor to accompany her to the pub. This outing was our only chance to have a talk. We soon gave up the church for the Tudor coffee room. There we irritated the waitress, by sitting for an hour over a single cup of coffee. This was all we could afford.

My other outing was usually to Redhill, where Mrs Noble had discovered an Italian hairdresser who spoke French. Once a week, I was free for the rest of the day, after I had cleared the breakfast dishes. On one such a trip, I wandered into the bookshop, which I had noticed on previous occasions. I asked the middle-aged man behind the counter, if he sold French books. He answered so fast that I did not understand what he said, and told him so. He just said "One moment" as he disappeared to the back of the shop. He returned bringing with him a much younger man. He introduced himself as Andre Pabre from Yverdon. Andre was on a two-year secondment, to learn English bookselling. I had met two Pabres dairymen while in Yverdon, and soon discovered that they were this young man's elder brothers. On the strength of this, Andre invited me to lunch in a nearby restaurant. He warned me that the food was quite disgusting, which it was. The meat was like shoe leather and the vegetables were overcooked and sodden in water.

But even if the food had been delicious, I would have had trouble eating it. As I walked in the restaurant, I had a very troubling experience of "déjà vu". This had never happened to me before. The restaurant was nearly full, which prompted Andre to suggest we go through to the back dining room, the door of which was closed. I found myself saying. "Yes, there is such a lovely view of the garden there. My companion asked me if I had been there before. At my negative reply, he looked quite puzzled. Andre opened the door, the room had a French window, which gave an unobstructed view of a beautiful garden. I was so disturbed that I was unable to eat. My companion did not seem to notice, and remained his urbane self throughout the meal. He offered to accompany me to London, if I could get some free time when the bookshop was closed.

On our first joint expedition to the capital, Andre took me to the National Gallery.

On that first visit, I was overwhelmed by the beauty of Verrochio's painting, *Tobia and the Angel*. I was also moved by Bellini's *Madonna of the Meadow*. Andre had a way of speaking lyrically about the pictures, which was infectious and inspiring. I did not feel that I was being taught to look, but of course, I was.

These visits were soon followed by matinee concerts at the Festival and the Albert Hall. I had not had the joy of hearing classical music, since Father Renouf played his 78 records for us at the orphanage.

The most memorable day was the one we spent in Holland Park. An open-air exhibition of sculpture, revived the emotion I had once felt in Yverdon. There I had wandered almost by accident, into the chateau where Rodin masterpieces were exhibited. I had been overwhelmed by their beauty. In Holland Park, I started a lifelong love affair with the work of the sculptress Elisabeth Frink.

After one of our visits to the National Gallery, we went to have tea at Lyons corner house, near Charing Cross station. He was concerned by my unhappy state, and gently led me to talk. I went on for several hours about the misery of my present situation, the events, which had led me to leave Switzerland so precipitously, and my miserable childhood, this in veiled terms. I had already told him that my ambition had been to study law and literature, so he suggested that I should use the time in my Kentish isolation to write.

But when I started to write, what came out on paper was not the recent events as one could have expected. It was my life with my mother, my disappointment at my father's defection, and the frustrations of orphanage life.

I showed Andre carefully selected extracts of the manuscript. He was encouraging. even enthusiastic about my efforts. It was a great moral booster. However, this was not enough to stop me on the road to psychological collapse. I was so nervous, that my clumsiness and absent-mindedness reached new proportions. On Christmas Day I broke a very precious cup. This was part of a fine porcelain set, which had been designed to celebrate the birth of the Princess Margaret Rose. Each piece was inscribed with the name of the Royal lady and her date of birth. Another day I dropped a two-pint bottle of milk on the doorstep. One evening, that the men did not come home for dinner, I left a rice pudding in the Aga overnight.

To each one of these incidents, Mrs Noble reacted hysterically. She cried and wiped the tears off her face with a big handkerchief, in a most dramatic fashion.

But the incident which brought the thunder on my head was caused by my loose tongue. I had kept in touch with Lilly, who was informing me of her efforts to get the Catholic church to allow her marry Mister David. Because she was keeping in touch with Mrs Noble, I had not written a word of criticism to her about the family.

One day, the lady, for once in a very jolly mood, informed me that her elder son had become engaged to a wealthy divorcee. Before I had time to think, it just came out. I said, "Lilly will be very upset". Mrs Noble expressed surprise. She wanted to know what about her son's engagement would make Lilly unhappy. I told her that I had been told that the two of them had been secretly engaged for some time. The lady was apoplectic, as if HER son would marry a servant! I was called a liar by everyone. Even Lilly accused me of having fabricated the whole story. I then understood why in her letters, she always referred to the secret engagement as "her little problem with the church". I had not kept any of her letters. I systematically destroyed all the mail, which came from Switzerland since receiving the abusive post.

The last attack on my emotional stability came from my stepmother. I had decided to stop the endless flow of begging letters, which I had received from her since I had left France. In an attempt to do so, I had answered her last demand by telling her that as an *au pair* I had no salary, my only income being £2 a week pocket money. It meant that I was no longer able to help her. The answer came swiftly in the form of an extremely insulting, and very long letter. According to her I was responsible for all the ills of her life, from her marital discord to her inability to feed her children correctly. I was unable to decipher some passages because of her poor spelling. Most of the content was written phonetically, but I was very distressed. Andre, whom I telephoned, advised me to destroy the letter. And then to write to Justine that I never wanted to hear from her again. Which I did.

On our next meeting, Andre strongly advised me to leave the Noble's house. He had already found me another post, in the house of the bookseller who employed him. After a short interview the Matthew family offered me the job, and a week later I moved to Surrey.

I had felt unable to tell Mrs Noble of my impending departure. I knew that I could not cope with her hysterics. So I gave my notice to her husband. At first, he did not take my claim of unhappiness seriously. He said that this was impossible, and exclaimed in French "Les francais sont un people gay, aimant la dance et les vins legers". I had taken the precaution of waiting until Mrs Noble had retired for the night to speak to her husband. I did not see her until the next morning. She informed me that the cause of my unhappiness was my selfishness. "If you gave a thought to other people, you would not be unhappy", she said.

Chapter Seventeen

The Matthew's home was very different from the mansion I had just left, and so were its inhabitants. The house was a large semi-detached Edwardian construction. Books lined all the available wall space of the sitting room, and of the bedrooms, often spilling on the floor. Even my room had a large empty set of shelves waiting to be filled. In the whole house the furniture was restfully shabby, and comfortable. There was no television in the sitting room, but a piano, a record player and piles of classical records in boxes and on the floor.

The workload was very light, compared with the demands, which had been made on me in the Noble's household. A cleaner came daily to do the heavy work. After I had cleared up the breakfast dishes my work was to make the beds, tidy and dust the bedrooms in preparation for Mrs Morgan to clean the floors. The first day I ran through the work, then came downstairs. Mrs Morgan asked me if I needed help with anything. I told her that I was finished upstairs. She took me aside, and told me that I was far too fast; no one doing this work ever came down for at least another hour and to please go back to the bedroom floors. So I did, and to kill time I started to read a few pages of a book in all the rooms. I looked up unknown words in the many dictionaries I found on the shelves.

The Matthews were a large extended family. Andre's employer Bernard was the bachelor uncle. His sister Margery had married another bookseller, Joseph Brown. They had two growing boys, and an adopted daughter. Janet was a magazine editor, who lived in London during the week.

The household was dominated by Mrs Matthew senior, a woman of over 80. She was bedridden after a stroke, but did not conform to the idea one may have of a cardiovascular victim. Every morning her daughter attended to her toilette. The matriarch then sat up in bed, and from there ruled the whole family. A side of her face was a little distorted since her illness, but she appeared to have no other visible sign of the stroke. She took herself to the lavatory without help, but never stayed out of bed longer than the needs of nature demanded.

Mrs Matthew read numerous books, as well as the New Statesman and Tribune every week. She listened to the BBC Home service, never missing a political programme. She loved "Any questions" as did all the other adult members of the family. At the end of the weekly broadcast, we all went to her bedroom. There, fortified by a cup of tea made by her son-in-law, they argued about it. During the period of the great "Bevanite crisis" about unilateral nuclear disarmament, this pacifist family enjoyed many lively discussions. These atheists worshipped at the altar of Saint Anthony Wedgwood Ben, and were enraged by Lady Violet Bonham Carter's Liberal views.

The two women also listened to Mrs Dale's Diary, while drinking their afternoon tea. The programme caused Mrs Matthew much enjoyable irritation. She was, however, even more exercised by the endless quarrelling in "The Archers".

For a while, I read Alice in Wonderland to Mrs Matthew in the afternoon. She stopped me, corrected my pronunciation every few words. I ended up getting frustrated. She then decided, that she would read to me instead, if I agreed to have English lessons with a relative of the family. Listening to Mrs Matthew's reading was a delight. I cannot read Dickens without hearing her voice in my head. I was also treated to books about Communist China, Inside Buchmanism, Katherine Mansfield's short stories, Uncle Tom's Cabin and much more.

Realising I was a keen reader, the English teacher lent me her copy of the original edition of Virginia Wolf's Orlando. This mark of trust touched me. Such a precious volume! Each lesson ended with discussing the book, which she had allowed me to take away. I loved the theme of it, even if I still found the style a challenge. I was delighted when Andre told me that he was unable to decide who the greatest writer in the English language of the century was, James Joyce or Virginia Wolf.

The family never left me out of their discussions. Because of this intensive education, my knowledge of the English language improved very fast. I was never allowed to be without an opinion on the subject under scrutiny. Sometimes I found the pressure more than I could cope with. In so far as I shared their left wing views, I did not quarrel with the fundamentals of Socialism. I never had the opportunity before of exploring these ideas, even in French. My political education had been limited to a short explanation by my stepmother, about the right and the left political parties.

I was very delicate, but I worked hard to keep up a front. I hoped no one would suspect that I had been so near breaking down. I was still struggling with the after effect of the recent happenings. At the end of difficult days, I said to myself, "That is another day survived, and tomorrow will be better". With no other help than Andre's support, gradually I did improve.

The food was the main obstacle to my physical recovery. I was still painfully thin, after seven months of near starvation. There was always plenty of food on the table, but it was on the whole, rather awful. The Matthew family were vegetarians. I found a lot of the dishes, indigestible or unpalatable. Whole Spanish onions boiled with potatoes, and served with a cheese sauce gave me abdominal cramps. Mashed yellow lentils dished out on a bed of pastry, and accompanied by the unavoidable boiled potatoes, did not go down too well either. But I was so glad to have plenty to eat that I chewed my way through everything that was put in front of me.

On my days off, I often made for the nearest restaurant. I usually ordered a meat dish, or fish and chips and bread and butter. Once, while in the Quality Inn eating house in Regent Street with Andre, I did not join him in ordering a dessert. I demanded instead another serving of fish and chips. The staff thought that because of my halting English, I had not realized that I had made a mistake. After a few words from Andre, they understood that I meant to have a second helping. By then, all the serving staff, and numerous customers were staring at me. The thought came into my head of lifting my jumper, to show the onlookers that my skirt was held up with pins. But one look at my friend sitting primly upright, and looking like such a gentleman, told me that it would be a mistake.

Andre was indeed a perfect gentleman. Our relationship remained at all times, one in which he acted as my mentor in cultural matters. He was my supporting friend, and my confidante. He never attempted to get close to me as a woman, and I began to think that it was either because I was so unattractively thin, or due to my fragility. Mrs Matthew began to say that I should not spend all my free time with Andre, who at 32 was too old for me. He would be going back to Zurich in a few months in any case. The family encouraged me to join the International Friendship League, which had a lively branch in Epsom.

There I met a friendly, cosmopolitan crowd of people of all ages. I was pursued by a young English man, Derek Black. In an effort to find out if Andre's apparent reluctance to approach me physically proved that there was something wrong with me, I began a flirtation. I told Andre that I had met another young man, but I did not get the slightest reaction from him. However, this budding romance came to an abrupt end before even the first kiss, when Derek sent me a letter in the most atrocious French, which ended with the comment that he hoped it was not too intellectual for me. I was furious, and even told Mrs Brown. She told me that they knew the arrogant young man. They had sacked him from one of their bookshops recently.

The person who benefited from my investigations into my desirability as a woman was a young German. Herman had tried to date me before the Black fiasco. Now, I decided to forget about his nationality because he was a very attractive man. We were soon engaged in frequent sessions of very heavy petting, which we just managed to keep under control. It was not always easy, but keeping it under control we did, as it seemed to be what he also wanted. He must have had his own agenda, as he was usually the one who managed the situation.

As the time for Andre to return to Switzerland approached, I became more anxious to sort out what stood between him and his inability to love me. One evening after we had spent the day pleasurably in London, he accompanied me to the bus stop. Seeing a vehicle disappearing round the corner, I suddenly feared that I had missed the last bus home. I put my hand on his arm, upon which he moved away quickly, as if he had been touched by fire. I felt very hurt, but of course, said nothing.

The following Sunday, we were having afternoon tea in my room. Andre suddenly told me that he just had a bad week. On my asking him the reason for this, he said that he feared that on the previous Sunday, he had been seen having a kiss and sharing a hug with a man in a park. As homosexuality was a criminal offence in England, he had been expecting the police to arrive at the shop or at his lodging all week. I reeled under the shock of Andre's revelations. For a moment the whole room was a blur. I looked out of the window, concentrating my attention on the garden below, and soon regained my composure. Two thoughts went through my head, I must not make him feel rejected, and I must not lose him. I asked him why he had not mentioned his sexual orientation before. He replied that I had been through such a difficult time. He had waited until I was strong enough to deal with this.

The next day I rang him at the shop and just said, "I only wanted to say hello!" He said that he knew why I had called, and that he really appreciated it.

Homophobia was at that time at its peak in England. Some prominent men had been caught frolicking on Brighton beach, and a trial was on the way. To commemorate the centenary of Oscar Wilde's birth, several of his plays were performed. This was to the disgust not only of Mrs Matthew, but of many people who disapproved of the author.

After he had discussed his homosexuality with me, I discovered a side of Andre which had until then been totally unknown to me. He thought his sexual orientation was decided by two important happenings in his childhood.

He was the youngest of a very large family, and had a very pampered early childhood. He was very close to his mother, and had a string of elder sisters who fussed over him continually. At the age of ten, when he was diagnosed to be suffering from bone tuberculosis, he was sent to a sanatorium in Leysin. The hospital was too far from home for frequent family visits. He cried for his beloved mother for several days.

Then came the realisation that loving was just too painful. He decided never to expose himself to missing anyone ever again.

When after two years he left the sanatorium, he found the whole atmosphere at home had changed. His previously jolly sisters had gone very quiet, and his mother always looked sad. He began to think that perhaps they were not pleased to have him back home. He soon changed his mind, finding everyone as affectionate towards him as they had always been, only in a more subdued way. Then one day when the family was out, he went though his parents' desk. He had seen his mother locking it up, which was never done before. He saw where she hid the key, and he retrieved it. And there in a drawer was the answer to his puzzlement. Legal documents told him that shortly after he had been admitted to the sanatorium, his father had been arrested and was condemned to serve a two-year prison sentence for raping the village idiot. He had only been released, shortly before Andre's return home. The shock was terrible and the twelve-year-old boy decided that, if being a man meant hurting mothers, he would have nothing to do with it. He then understood why his father never ate with the family now, but had his plate taken to his workshop by one of his sisters.

I was now able to see Andre as a person in his own right, not just as a fulfiller of my needs. I cared for him more than ever, but it was in a different way. He once pointed out that now I was always the one to ask how he was before he had time to enquire about my wellbeing.

As he was so near to returning home, he talked more about his friends in Zurich. The name Elizabeth appeared frequently in the conversation. I had heard about this woman often since I knew Andre. At times, I had thought that she was someone he had been in love with. Telling me the story of the relationship now was something of a warning to me. He had worked with Elizabeth in the bookshop for some years. She was unhappily married, and had a child with serious behavioural problems. Andre befriended her and they became very close. She eventually left her husband. She put her child in a Rudolf Steiner boarding school. She had thought that her marital situation was making it impossible for Andre to declare himself. After five years, she could no longer stand the wait and wrote telling him so. In his answer, he told her about his sexual orientation. She was devastated, but the friendship survived.

After Andre's return to Zurich my morals took a serious dip. Without his support and humour, my mood became rather erratic. I found it hard to keep up a reasonable front now, when I did not feel cheerful. The endless challenging discussions of the Matthews irritated me, when I was not up to them. The mornings were the hardest. However, as the day progressed I felt better, even after a bad start. One day Mrs Morgan had not come to work. I was asked to clean the grate, and start the fire in Mrs Matthew's room. I was not feeling at my best when the old lady started an argument. She asked, "Do you believe in the immaculate conception?" Thinking I could curtail the conversation, I replied, "I don't know, I haven't thought about it". Well! That really was the wrong answer. I was subjected to a tirade about the importance of having an opinion on the matter. When she eventually allowed me to reply, I told her that, as a lapsed Roman Catholic I did not feel concerned. I added that when I belonged to the faith, I was not allowed to think for myself, so I did not, and quickly left the room.

I had promised Andre that when I had fulfilled my contact at the Matthews, I would try to get a job in a bookshop in London. By pulling strings at the Home Office, my employers had succeeded in getting me a working permit for eighteen months, instead of the usual year. But after fourteen months, I felt that I could honourably leave if an opportunity presented itself. I applied for a post at Hachette, the French bookshop in Regent Street, and was lucky enough to be offered a job. I had told the Matthews of my plans. When the offer of the job came, I gave them my notice to quit. I had, by then, decided that I wanted to stay in England permanently. But to be sure this was really what I wanted, I felt I should go back to Switzerland once. I could then return a suitcase my aunt had lent me, and spend time with Andre.

When I had started work at the Matthews they offered me a salary of £3 a week. After a few days stay, I felt it was an unfair sum. My workload was very light, compared with the exhausting day I had at the Nobles, where I was paid a weekly £2. So I negotiated my salary downwards, and in the end accepted £2.10 shillings. When I left the

Matthews after 14 months, I asked for two weeks' holiday money. Mrs Brown told me it was dishonest on my part to expect it. As a domestic worker, I was not entitled to any annual leave pay. Mrs Morgan did not get any holiday money either. So much for militant socialists!

I had become very friendly with a French girl I had met at the International Friendship League. When she moved to West London we kept in touch. The widowed lady for whom Josette worked had offered me hospitality when I returned from Switzerland. This would give me time to look for accommodation. I gave this address to Hachette so they could inform me when the working permit was granted, and give me a starting date.

Chapter Eighteen

The first thing I did when I arrived to Switzerland was to go straight to La Sarraz to return my aunt's suitcase. Her welcoming remark was that I need not have bothered. She did not need the case, and had not expected to get it back. In view of the poor opinion the family had of me, it had seemed important to return it. She had made it an issue on lending it to me, which she seemed to have forgotten.

When questioned as to the date of my return to Switzerland, I replied that I had now moved to London where I could go to advanced English classes. There was no point in returning until my knowledge of the language was good enough to help me secure a good job. Aunt Theresa joined us for tea, then the two of them sang a duo to the tune of "what a pity, you did not marry Nicholas"! When I had decided to go to England in such a precipitous manner, I had told Aunt Anna all about the episode with Mr Pinnard's senior. I did this to explain the need I felt to get away for a while. To my amazement she had said that it was a pity I had not told her about it. She would have taken me to the family solicitor, Maitre Kitchener, who would have sorted it out for me. She had even said, "Why do you behave as though you had no family?" I was glad to have had, for once, a reasonably sympathetic response from my aunt. So I had thought it better not to reply provokingly.

When I visited Aunt Anna she pressed me to stay for a few days. I thought it was too late in our history for her to offer me a bed. My heart was hardened. I was just going through the formalities of politeness to make my exit easier. What I really wanted was to go to Zurich and see Andre. My aunt's sad face did not touch me.

Andre met me accompanied by his flat mate, and lover. Walter was very much older than Andre. He spoke very little French, so communication between us was very limited. I knew that the pair had lived in the tiny flat Walter had rented while Andre was in England. I was booked a room in a luxury flat nearby. As soon as I set foot in Switzerland, my digestive system went on overdrive. I did not have any pain, but everything I ate went straight through me.

I could not enjoy visiting Zurich. Depression, overcame me the moment I found myself alone in my lodgings. This time I could not talk to Andre about my feelings, as he was the reason for my misery. He seemed, in any case, totally oblivious of the hell I was going through. He worked in the bookshop six days a week, so I was alone most of the day. I sometimes met him for lunch, and we spent every evening together, but the days were long.

Occasionally, I went to the bookshop long before it was due to shut for the midday break. On one of these occasions Elizabeth invited me to share lunch with her. During the course of the meal, she talked about herself very frankly. She told me that her love for Andre had stood in the way of her trying to sort out her marital problems. Her husband wanted to seek help, but she refused. She felt guilty about that, almost as much as she did to have sent her son to boarding school. She had mistakenly thought Andre would come to her if she were free. She had noticed my unhappiness, and urged me to return to England as soon as possible. Elizabeth said to me gently, "Do not waste your life hoping for an outcome, which will never take place". I took her advice very seriously. It did not seem to come from a jealous woman, but out of a genuine concern for me. Seeing her still so unhappy was, in any case, enough for the message to be accepted and understood.

When I met Andre that evening he gave me a letter, which Josette had forwarded from Hachette. The Home Office had refused their application to employ me on the grounds that I had not been in the United Kingdom long enough. I was still only allowed to work as a domestic or hospital worker. I was by then anxious to get back to England. I telephoned Josette and asked her to scan the numerous advertisements for *au pair* girls, which appeared in the evening papers. The next day she called me that she had found me a post in a family, a few minutes from her own address.

Chapter Nineteen

The Pipping family lived in a large Regency house, on the good side of Hammersmith bridge. The husband, Jack an architect was English, his wife Anita was a South American Jewish beauty. They had two children, Nicola who was nearly five; and a toddler, Adrian, who walked but did not speak. The two top floors of the house were let, one to a Jewish doctor and his wife, and the other to a symphonic orchestra fiddle player.

As soon as I walked in the house I felt at ease. Anita Pipping was welcoming and friendly. She seemed a little nervous when she began to describe what my duties would be. The mornings were to be fairly straightforward. It was when it came to telling me what I had to do in the afternoons, that her nervousness increased. I was prepared for the worst. She told me that everyday I had to pick up Nicola from school after lunch. The two of us would travel on a bus to Oxford Street. I should then take the child to the Institute of Psychoanalysis in New Cavendish Street, wait for 50 minutes and bring her home. Mrs Pipping was quite unprepared for my reaction. She had just parted from a German *au pair* who was totally against psychoanalysis. The girl had constantly shown her discontent at having to inflict this treatment on a child. I had been wishing for some time, that I could afford to have analytical help myself. I was able to express my genuine understanding to Mrs Pipping.

The deal was the best I had had so far. Most weeks I enjoyed being free Saturday afternoon and all of Sunday. During the week, I finished work after I had cleared up the children's high tea. I had to baby sit occasional evenings. When I had made friends, they were allowed to spend the evening with me; so staying in was not a hardship. I was paid the princely sum of £3 a week.

I looked rather frumpish, as I never thought much about what I wore. I had been dressed for so long in second hand clothes that were usually too old for me. I had no idea at all how to build up a smart wardrobe, on any budget. Mrs Pipping took the improvement of my appearance seriously. I told her that I was too hard up to be elegant, so she set out to prove me wrong. I saved up for a few weeks, and we went on a shopping expedition to Hammersmith. She taught me about colour matching and coordination of style. She screamed like a banshee when having taken the colour idea literally, I was proposing to match a thick polo neck jumper with a lightweight summer skirt, because the two garments were blue. I did learn, and very fast. The greatest compliment Anita paid me, was after a party she had given. She said she had found it hard to believe, that the elegant young woman who was offering canapés to her guests, was the dowdy girl who had walked through her door a few months earlier.

The mornings were very busy as I had the sole guard of the little boy, while cleaning the part of the house lived in by the family. The tenants cleaned inside their own flats, but I had to keep the stairs spotless. There was also a mountain of ironing. I did no cooking, having being schooled by Josette to say I did not have the know how.

Every day Mrs Pipping took Nicola to school, and then disappeared for the rest of the morning. She came home in time to prepare lunch. I knew she did not have a job, and I became very curious as to what she did five times a week. Some days, she was in a state of abstraction when she came home. I soon began to suspect that she too was having psychoanalysis. This was confirmed one lunch time. I heard the tenant Dr. Meyer asking my employer "How is Dr. Peters?" She answered "Beautiful as ever", and they both laughed. When the visitor had gone she told me that Dr. Peters was her psychoanalyst.

This conversation seemed to have given her the opening she was waiting for. She continued by saying she had noticed that when I thought myself unobserved, I often looked depressed. I could not deny it, but said I was getting gradually better. I added that I could not afford the psychoanalytic help I needed. She agreed that individual psychoanalysis, was obviously beyond my budget but there may be a way of getting me free help, if I accepted to have therapy in a group. She happened to have an application form in the house, which her husband had refused to use. I readily agreed to apply, and filled in the form.

The French analyst, I met at the Psychotherapy Clinic drew from me the story of my miserable childhood. I gave him the catastrophic details of my employment record. I kept on about my fear of dismissal, which was the plague of my life. The interview ended with the analyst's comment that he could not put me in a group because I was too fragile. In his opinion "The other members of the group would make mincemeat of you, they would use your lack of fluency in English to crush you". And that was that, well almost.

A few weeks later I received a letter from a Social Worker at the Psychotherapy Clinic. She was offering me an interview. But I was about to leave London with the Pipping family for a two-week holiday so I ignored it. So much had happened in the house since I had seen the analyst. There was no space in my head, for my more personal concerns.

The Myers were a very friendly couple who, soon after my arrival invited me to their flat. I quickly became aware that all was not well with Rachel Myers' health. She had a little dry cough, which had increased in intensity very rapidly. One day, I was sitting on the children's swing at the bottom of the garden. On looking towards the house, my eyes fell on the Myers's open kitchen window. They were both sitting at the table, Rachel was crying and her husband was comforting her. I came off the swing instantly. I felt that I had opened the wrong door. I never mentioned the incident to the Pippins. But a dreadful fear entered my mind. I sensed that Rachel's distress had to do with her cough. A few days later, I saw her leaving the house to go to the LSE, where she was an assistant lecturer. She looked broken. The awful thought came to my mind, that she was going to die. I tried to dismiss it, but it would not go away. She was soon admitted to hospital, and three weeks later, died. Cancer of the lungs had killed her at the age of 35; the same age that Louisa had been when we lost her.

An opaque fog fell on the house. Everybody was deeply distressed. But no one seemed able to connect with another person, and be comforted by the sharing of the sorrow. It was as if all the residents of the house took Rachel's death very hard, but felt alone in their grief. Noah Myers went to stay with friends for a few days. Bob Pipping who was already leading a semi-detached life, was even more absent than usual. Anita cried loudly, but alone in her bedroom. Janet Smith, the fiddle player who lived on the top floor, disappeared totally for a while.

I stayed home to look after the children while all the adults went to Golders Green for Rachel's funeral. Anita had told Nicola that they were going to say goodbye to Rachel. Seeing them all dressed in formal wear, the child had asked if they were going to a party. Her mother's answer had the effect of sending the little girl into one of her tantrums. Because she thought that I preferred her baby brother there were moments when Nicola was unable to accept help from me. That day try hard as I may, I could not calm her. The child needed her mother. She referred to me at all times as "the horrible nasty beast". Even her morning greeting was "Good morning, you horrible nasty beast". This negative attitude made it very difficult for me to comfort her.

As the same epithet was given to her analyst, I did not take the insult to heart. She was an unhappy five-year-old child, not just the little monster she appeared to be. I did try to keep this in mind, when she was screaming on the top of the 73 Bus all the way from Barnes to Hammersmith, if I was lucky, or Kensington High Street, if I was not. "I don't want to go to Mr Joseph, I don't like him, he is a horrible nasty beast." only to give her therapist an affectionate greeting when she met him. On the bus, the passengers were divided between the people who thought she was funny, and those who were concerned. After a few weeks of oscillating between ignoring and scolding her, I found that bribery worked best. I kept sweets in my bag, to which she had access when she cooperated. During her session, I tried to have a little rest in the waiting room. She started leaving her therapist and hiding her head in my lap screaming "Protect me from that from that horrible man". I was advised to go out of the clinic, and I became a regular customer of the coffee shops in Marylebone High Street.

The journey home was not often without its surrealistic moments. If the bus was full Nicola had to sit on my lap, which she resented. When a man sat next to us, she would try to embarrass me by asking very loudly a variation of "Have you got two big fat breasties?" or if I demanded that she stop kicking my shins with her heels, it would be a remark of the type "If you do not behave yourself, I will take you out of the bus with no clothes on at all", raising her voice as she got to the end of the sentence. I usually stared out of the window to avoid the amused looks of my fellow passengers.

The Pippins had rented a flat in Folkestone, and soon after Rachel Myers's funeral we set off for two weeks holidays. All the adults were depressed that the couple was breaking up. They were barely speaking to each other. I had been unable to cry, or show any sign of grief. I felt that everyone would think my sorrow was inappropriate. I had known the Myers such a short time, so I kept my sadness hidden. After a few days in the gloomy Folkestone flat, everyone's mood became very erratic. It was at its worse, on the days the weather was not good enough to be spent on the beach. I was feeling unwell, and soon developed a raging fever. Anita Pippins was phobic about germs. She could not cope with illness. She took the family to the beach, leaving me alone all day. When they returned in the evening, Nicola came to my room and greeted me with "I hate you, I wish you were dead instead of Rachel". I began weeping in a sorrow where all the losses of my life, and my hopeless situation were all mixed up. The next day my temperature was back to normal. I was still shaken, and prone to bursting into tears. I told Anita that I needed to have another quiet day. She was none too pleased. But that day, I was glad to see them all go to the beach. This allowed me some reflective time. By the time the family returned, I had decided to contact the Social worker recommended by Dr Martin, on our return to London.

I was cleaning the stairs, and was interrupted by Noah Myers, on his way down. He apologized for disturbing my work. I replied tartly. "Yes, and such intellectual work at that!" He sat on the steps and said to me. "You are unhappy because you are doing work which is far below your capacity". Not, you are sulky, awkward, moody, but unhappy. He added that Rachel had thought I was someone very special, I was moved. Here were two people, for whom I had the greatest esteem, who thought I was a worthwhile person. In that instant, I had the sudden revelation that my desperate situation was the cause of my misery, not a sign of moral depravity. These few minutes changed my life.

To my amazement, this view of my employment record was confirmed by the social worker, I eventually met at the Psychotherapy Clinic. When I gave her the long list of jobs I had failed to retain in the last few years, her immediate reaction was. "Well, none of these jobs were exactly good jobs" which I took to mean good jobs for you

I had further talks with Noah Myers. He repeated that Rachel had been very impressed by me. She thought I was not the usual sort of au pair, but a person with great depth and potential. Before he moved out of the house, he gave me two of his wife's precious books of French poetry. I regarded this gift as tangible proof of the couple's regard.

Chapter Twenty

After a year at the Pippins, I was buoyed up by the support I was getting from Noah Myers and Ms Casters, the social worker. I decided to try my luck again with the Home Office. I had lived in England just over three years, and felt I had a chance. I advertised in the Bookseller Journal, for a post in a bookshop or a publishing office. Despite being very frank about my lack of experience, I received many offers, both from bookshops and publishers. As I was unable to assess them, Ms Casters arranged for me to meet the head of a publishing firm she knew. This kind man worked his way through the pile of replies. He discarded a few but left me with a substantial list of potential employers. Notwithstanding his short acquaintance with me, he suggested I could give his name as a reference should I need the help.

The first publisher I applied to called me for an interview for the post of junior clerk. After a spelling test I was offered the job at a salary of £6 a week. Mr Parks' application to the Home Office was successful. Anita Pippins was by now separated from her husband and was anxious to increase her income. She fitted the so far unused extension to the house into a bedsit room for me. At the cost of £2.5 shillings a week, I had at last a little home of my own, and my independence.

Nicola's attitude towards me softened. I was no longer the "horrible, nasty beast" but became "You". When I responded to her, "Good morning you" by "Good morning to you, too", she improved her greeting to "Good morning to you one", which she kept up until she grew bored with the game.

But it was the little boy who contributed to keeping my links with the family close. Adrian was now nearly 3 years old, and he still did not speak. The family thought he may be mentally retarded, but I knew he was not. I knew he understood everything that went on around him. His mother teased me for what she took to be my blindness to my little darling. Adrian and I were very attached to each other. When I moved into the extension, he turned up every morning with his clothes in his arms, wanting me to dress him. When I came back from the office, he would be waiting for me. Most weekends, I took him out at least once, either to feed ducks at the pond in Barnes or for a bus ride. He was always very happy to go. But as soon as he realized we were on the way home, he sat on the pavement and refused to budge. When he started to speak his first full sentence was "go to feed the ducks", which he uttered everywhere and in whatever the context. Then he seemed to go straight from being totally silent, to full grammatical adult speech overnight. This was to the dismay of his family, who had declared him to be backwards. I did not have the generosity to keep quiet about having being right, but gloated relentlessly. Nicola paid me one of her rare spontaneous visits to declare, "Mummy said, she thinks you think you are god".

My relationship with Anita Pippins had never been one of mistress and servant. It was not her style, despite having being brought up in a household with staff. Social barriers fell down, when I expressed my understanding about the family's involvement in psychoanalysis. It was not exactly a situation of equals that existed between us. Anita was too competitive a person for that. But a position of equilibrium could be maintained, so long as I accepted that I was not and could never be top dog; and would never have anything better than she had. She never ceased to remind me that Dr. Peters was one of the country's top analyst, while I saw a social worker "just for support". To be sure, I never forgot the difference of treatment we both got. She always referred to Ms Casters as Auntie Casters. While Rachel Myers was alive, Anita mentioned several times that "Poor Rachel" could only afford to see an analyst twice a week, as opposed to the five times she herself was able to finance. She always forgot to mention that Rachel financed her own analytical sessions, while it was her own mother who paid the bill.

She could be very generous, both with the giving of her time and gifts. Only occasionally, she had an irrational outburst of stinginess. She made a scene because I had bought eggs bigger than she had instructed me to do, and a better quality of margarine than she wanted. When I made a sandwich for Noah Myers to accompany a cup of tea soon after his wife's death, she said my extravagance was the cause that she would soon have to live her off her capital. As I had not understood what that meant, I had to ask Noah. He explained that rich people lived on the interest financial institutions paid them on the money they had invested. Unfortunately, he had overheard Anita's reprimand to me. It was what made him leave the house, to my chagrin.

I started my new life with excitement, but also with trepidation. Parks was a small firm started a few years earlier by an ambitious young man. Mr Parks' keenness to succeed, and his knowledge of the book world created an atmosphere of dynamism and never ending surprises. Every day the boss read most newspapers before coming to the office. He usually arrived around eleven o'clock. By then, his secretary had already scanned the papers herself, and noted items, which could be of interest. This meant ferreting out potential new writers, reviews of past publications and any other relevant articles.

My work included manning the small switchboard, registering unsolicited manuscripts, sending the publicity material to wholesalers, packing and expediting review copies to the relevant journalists. I learned to assist the senior secretary Fredericka, in the numerous tasks, which came under the heading of book production. I made coffee in the morning, and tea in the afternoon and seemed to be forever dashing across the road to the local post office.

If Mr Parks thought he had found a pearl in the press, I would spend a large part of the day on the telephone. I had to track the person he was hoping to catch in his net. I very soon learned not to be intimidated by a grand name, or even an infamous one. I could be ringing Buckingham Palace one minute, and trying to trace a suspected Nazi criminal the next. Everyone with a modicum of topical interest was grist to the paper mill of the firm. Sometimes I was sent out to collect material at addresses all over central London. Many of these trips allowed me to meet people who were in the news. I visited literary figures, who would never come my way in any other context. I was sent to Gordon Square, to the house of surviving members of the Bloomsbury Group. I had been fascinated by these people ever since I had read *Orlando*. The lady in Epsom, who had been my English teacher, had told me so much about them. I was not to be disappointed; the sheer eccentricity of the household was a joy.

But working for Mr Parks was not always so joyful. He was a very mercurial man who was prone to bad moods. When he was particularly irate, Frederica was the only person who could weather the storm, and eventually calm it. She protected the office staff, although she could not always succeed in protecting the representatives. They always ended up getting the worst of the boss's temper. Mr Parks usually calmed down after he had sacked one of these unfortunate men, most of the time on a trumped up set of grievances. We consoled ourselves with the thought that he had never dismissed a woman. But when the only man left in the firm was the quiet editorial assistant, who shared a large office with the boss, I became very nervous. My anxiety increased when Fredericka who had recently married, announced that she was leaving the firm as she was pregnant. I said to her, "Your pregnancy does not show at all, so you still have a long way to go". "Don't you believe it", she replied laughingly, "It is the second baby which always takes nine months".

Fredericka was replaced by a bird like blond woman who was older than all of us. She was very formal with the rest of the staff, and did not appreciate the easygoing atmosphere, which existed on our side of the green baize door.

Because I was missing the relationship I had enjoyed with Fredericka I became closer to the accounts staff with whom I could at least exchange a few pleasantries daily. The subscription clerk Jenny was a very jolly Cockney, whose language I had sometimes trouble understanding, but whose humour delighted me. Our riotous laughter, invariably started Ms Ganing on her frequent refrain: "Hush chaps". Jenny had been entertaining us with the progress she was making learning to knit. When she had finished a garment for the child she was expecting, she announced it loudly to the whole office. I was not really listening to the conversation, so I asked absentmindedly "And did you try it on him? "No" she replied, "I did not have time". Everyone roared with laughter, except Ms Ganing who was furious.

After this incident the other members of the staff tried very hard to be quieter. I nursed resentment towards the woman. She had excluded me from the production side of the work, from the moment she arrived, so I would not oblige. I had tried to assist her in the creative aspect of the book's production. All my offer of help had been rejected. I was rather bored and very angry.

However, the secretary's stay in the firm was short. To keep the office open as many hours as possible, Mr Parks had arranged that the staff should have staggered working hours. Two of us started at 9.30, while all the others were due in the office by 9.00. Because the boss never turned up much before eleven, no one bothered too much about punctuality. One day, in the week before Christmas all the 9 o'clock staff arrived in the office between 9.10 and 9.15. They found Mr Parks already seated at his desk. I was due to arrive at 9.30, but turned up nearly five minutes late, just as the switchboard phone was ringing. My colleagues warned me to be quick. I answered the call as calmly as I could manage, with a cheery, "Good morning Mr Parks". Jenny was just walking in as the boss asked me if she was there. Hearing my positive reply, he ordered me to send all the staff into his office at once, apart from Jenny and myself.

They came out of the boss's office, having being reprimanded like naughty children. They were told that their unpunctuality would be punished by the loss of their Christmas bonus. The bonus may be paid at Easter, if their time keeping improved. The extra cash consisted only of one week's salary, but we all counted on it. Not risking to lose their job most of the staff took their punishment quietly, but Ms Ganing was extremely angry. She said it was not the loss of a few pounds that upset her. She resented, having being subjected to the humiliation of being carpeted like an underling. This proved just too much for her.

On her return from the Christmas holiday, she announced that she was leaving at the end of the week. When alone with me, she told me that my insolent attitude had contributed to her decision to go. Her last words to me were "You have amazing staying power." This sentence echoed in my head, as I remembered the failed nun at the orphanage. She had used these same words to me on leaving the order, and I suddenly felt very guilty.

In clearing up the drawers of her desk, I found some private papers, which she had left there, by accident or design. These documents were copies of letters sent to various financial institutions on behalf of her mother. We thus found out that Ganing was not her real name, but that she was a princess of German origin, judging by the Von, which came after the word princess. We understood why she found us commons. Not surprisingly, she had felt unable to accept the humiliation of being berated by Mr Parks.

I was to see her again almost twenty years later, in a sandwich bar in Wigmore Street. She had hardly changed. I was longing to go up to her and apologize for my past immature behaviour. I hesitated, and in an instant she was gone. I had missed my chance to make amends to her, and to shake off my guilt. I went back to that bar many times, but never saw her again. In the end, I consoled myself with the thought that she probably did not even remember me.

Ms Ganing was for a short while succeeded by a number of agency secretaries. They knew little about book production, and all of them enjoyed my help. I was thrilled to be allowed to phone the printers, and use the knowledge of the technical aspects of the work. However, this respite was only too short, as Mr Parks soon found the assistant he wanted. Ms Bort was a middle-aged woman, who came straight to Parks from a prestigious publishing house. She had been a secretary to a member of the Bloomsbury Group for some years.

But the disappointment was acute. Ms Bort was very unpleasant. She made it clear that she had only come to work for such a small firm, because her famous boss had just retired. She herself only had a few years left before retirement. She excluded me totally from the production part of the work. She was more brutal than Ms Ganing would ever have been. Ms Bort snatched the telephone from my hands, whenever she realized that I was taking a message from the printers, or talking to an author. But her worse flaw was the habit she had of repeating to Mr Timber everything that went on in the office. She could not say much about the account clerks, as she knew nothing about their work. But she twisted my deeds, to make me appear in a bad light. Fredericka had discovered, that I had a knack of making even the most reluctant authors sign piles of their book. Ms Bort told Mr Parks that I was too familiar with a celebrated sportsman whose biography the firm was publishing. One evening when I was still in the office, the green baize door was left open and I overheard the boss repeat this to the editorial assistant.

I had now worked for the firm nearly two years, and had become very efficient. I could do the routine tasks in a fraction of the time it had taken me at the beginning. It was at that moment, that Ms Bort chose to deprive me of the most interesting and creative part of the work. I was now seriously under-employed, but it was not appropriate for me to tackle the boss about this at that instant.

As frequently happened Mr Parks was engaged in one of his numerous legal battles. He was pursuing a ghost writer, who had in his estimation been too slow in delivering a manuscript. For weeks, every few days I was made to send a telegram to the unfortunate man to hurry him along. It was always the same wording, or almost. A well-respected journalist, the writer ended up having a nervous breakdown. He could not finish the book. The publisher demanded the return of the advance paid.

Mr Parks discovered that in one of the telegrams I had omitted the word "Yet". He announced to whoever could hear it, that this error would surely cost him the loss of the court case.

When the storm had abated, I asked for an interview with the boss. I told him that since Fredericka's departure from the firm, I had gradually become under employed. Neither Ms Ganing nor Ms Bort honoured the promise I had been given when joining the office, that I would be involved in the book production. Now that I had become more proficient in performing the routines tasks, I needed more work. When I repeated this to Ms Casters that evening, her irritated remark was, "How could you be so stupid?" The next day I knew that in her usual blunt way, she had been right.

The following morning Ms Bort spent an unusually long time closeted with Mr Parks. When she emerged, she asked me to swap lunch hour with her. As Jenny was absent that day, it meant the secretary would be alone to man the office for the hour. She usually disliked it, as she would have to do menial tasks such as manning the switchboard and coping with casual callers. At 12 I left the office with the account clerk, both of us wondering the meaning of the secretary's manoeuvre. My colleague had an idea that Ms Bort wanted us both out of the office. She wanted to do something, out of our sight, earshot or both.

On our return from lunch, I was summoned to Mr Parks' office. He handed me a long letter, in which he was giving me notice to quit. He referred to my dismissal as redundancy, resulting from a general reorganisation of the office. There was a long paragraph about my hard working qualities, my loyalty and my probity. To show his appreciation of my past endeavours, he was giving me a bonus of £40, and wishing me the very best for the future.

Verbally, he acknowledged that I had been let down by the firm, who had not kept its engagements towards me. He accepted that since Fredericka had left the firm, I had not been treated fairly and apologized. In view of this, he was not demanding that I work my week's notice. He invoked the London bus strike, which made moving around the town very difficult. He added that if I had not found a post by the end of the following week, he would take me back on the payroll, and try to give me a fairer deal.

When Ms Bort was out of the office, I showed the letter to the other clerk, and reported the conversation with the boss. She agreed that the £40 bonus, and the offer to take me back at the end of the following week did not make much sense. It was according to the senior clerk, Mrs Witton, a most unusual practice. It was also totally out of character with the way Mr Parks normally worked. I was too shocked to think, only conscious that I had brought this disaster on my own head.

After the other clerk left at 5 o'clock I was left alone with Ms Bort. She offered to buy me a coffee, and I felt unable to refuse. When we were sitting in the coffee house, her manner towards me totally changed. It was not the sharp, rasping woman I had in front of me, but a honeyed voice seductress. She was all kindness and sympathy, and offered me her friendship. I said I was all right, I did have plenty of friends. I knew only too well, that I could never be a friend of this woman; even if the two of us were the only human beings left on earth. But as she put her hand on mine, saying in a sugary tone, "I know you are lonely, I replied, "We are all lonely at times." She said. "You know that is not what I mean". Upon which I got up, and made a swift exit. As I walked to the bus stop, I told myself that whatever happened the following week, Ms Bort had made sure I could never go back to Parks.

At first, I thought that she had attempted to take advantage of my distress to try to seduce me. But I met a young woman at a dinner party, who had previously worked in the same firm as Ms Bort. She told me that the woman had been disliked for her spiteful tongue, and her jealousy of younger colleagues. My new acquaintance, did not agree with my view of what had prompted the woman to make a crude pass at me at that particular moment. In her opinion, it was more likely that Ms Bort had engineered the dismissal, which was not. This was just the kind of trickery she would indulge in. The purpose would have been of upsetting me, to the point I would be feeble enough to fall in her arms. She would be only too pleased to offer me support and consolation. If I had returned to the firm, I would have been putty in her hands. But her approach had been so obvious, that even in my distraught state I had seen through it.

The bonus and the reference to my loyalty were easily explained, once I had spoken to Frederica. It was meant as a reminder to keep my mouth shut, about an episode, which had taken place when she was still working in the firm, but in her absence. In line with Mr Parks' philosophy of keeping the office open as many hours as possible, a member of staff had to be on duty on Saturday morning. When it was considered that I was competent to be left alone, I was allowed to take my turn in fulfilling this task. Mr Parks did not usually come in, unless there was an item in the post, which demanded his urgent attention. But one Saturday morning when I arrived he was already there. After a cursory greeting, he asked me how long it would take me to wrap up and address the review copies of a new title. This book was due to be published the following week. I told him that the books were ready, as it had been my intention to post them early on Monday morning. He then ordered me to take all the volumes, which were to be posted outside the metropolitan area to the post office at once. I was then to deliver the rest by hand up and down the Fleet Street district. I was told to seek out the appropriate review editors, and try when possible not to leave the books at the reception desk. He then ordered a taxi, and sent me on my way without further explanation.

As it happened, only one review editor was at her desk. There was nothing I could do, but trust the rest of the books to the goodwill of receptionists. But I did meet the writer Nancy Spain; she expressed surprise and delight at having the book delivered by hand to her personally. "At least", she said "that one has not been stolen". I did not spoil her thrill, by telling her that all the other review editors would have had the same privilege had they been on duty.

It was only on Monday morning that I found out that Mr Parks had involved me in an illegal act. The book he was about to publish, recounted the problems the British Army had recently encountered with a Middle East ruler. The manuscript had been vetted by the War Office, and given the all clear. Four days before the book was due to be published, the Government had a change of mind, and decided to block the publication. Mr Parks' friendly spy at the War Office, had contacted him on Friday evening. He warned the boss that first thing on Monday morning a D/notice would be served. By then the author had been paid a substantial advance, the book was printed; at the trade counter the orders were ready for dispatch to the wholesalers and the bookshops. Mr Parks was not the man to sustain such a loss without a fight. Hence, the decision to flood the press with the work on Saturday. The D/notice would be useless once the book was not only all over Fleet Street but on its way around the world.

Publishers sent review copies to literary editors on days that suited them. There was nothing inherently suspicious about getting the volumes out to the press on the Saturday. At the time, Fredericka had explained it all to me in the strictest confidence. But she had not been too pleased that I had been used in this way. Now all she could do was offer me advice about the most likely agencies to offer me interviews in publishing firms. She was nursing her new baby, and had preoccupations of her own.

The employment agencies were quick at arranging interviews, but moving around London without buses was very arduous. I had instinctively always avoided using the Underground, but now there was no alternative. The stress of finding my way in the overcrowded stations, added to my anxiety. By Wednesday afternoon I had not been offered a post. I bought an evening paper, and over a cup of tea I scanned the adverts. There was a demand for a filing clerk at the Great Ormond Street Children's Hospital. As I was in the area, I was offered an interview that day. The hospital secretary who saw me was friendly, until I showed him Mr Parks' letter. His manner suddenly changed, and looking at me over his half moon spectacles he queried the £40 bonus, saying this smelled very strongly of money given in lieu of notice. What had I done to bring about instant dismissal? I suddenly understood why I had spent three days going to fruitless interviews. On Thursday, an agency arranged an appointment at a magazine publisher in the city. I did not show the letter and before I even left the building I was offered the post. All I had been asked to do was wait in an outer room, while the Personnel Officer telephoned Mr Parks. According to the accounts clerk, who contacted me that evening, my previous employer had been very complementary about my work. He had added that having started in the firm without any experience, I had by now outgrown the job. He wished me well.

The following Monday morning I stated work at Mediatic Periodicals Ltd., I had expected the work to be dull, and it was. I was stuck in the Subscription Dept, or should I say in the subscription shambles? But being without any other means of support but my own labour, I had been in a state of acute anxiety since I was sacked. By that Thursday morning, I would have accepted a job in the anti-chamber of hell, had one been offered. I did not take seriously the promises made by the Personnel Officer to let me know when an opening came up in a more creative part of the firm.

Chapter Twenty-One

Through Noah Myers I had been mixing socially with the "la crème de la crème" of the psychoanalytic world, as well as members of allied professions. I had thought for sometime that publishing was a rather shallow trade. I felt the need to work with people in a more meaningful way, but I did not yet know how. I had attended an evening course on experimental psychology at the evening Institute in Richmond. But giving neurosis to rats did not really appeal to me. I then registered for a series of public lectures on aspects of mental health. There I usually sat next to a friendly woman. One evening while waiting for the conference to start, she began a conversation, being rather intrigued by my presence there. I told her that I wanted to work with people, but did not think I had the basic qualifications to be accepted for a course of study. Also I was not yet sure which way I wanted to go. She suggested I started by doing voluntary social work to acquire some experience. This may have helped me decide what to do next. Faced with the need I had to keep a roof over my head, she thought that the LCC's Children Care Office could use me to supplement the professional workers. This organisation, which looked after the welfare of London's school children, always needed voluntary workers. They helped the professional workers by visiting the homes of single-parent families in the evenings. The single mothers were often working in the daytime. This kind woman had given me an introduction to the head of the Wandsworth office. There, after an introduction to the professional workers, and the allocation of a supervisor, I was accepted on the team.

This was really my introduction to the British working class, and to its way of life. Because of the very specific nature of the referrals the catchment area was extensive. While the bulk of the visits were on the Alton Estate in Roehampton. I had to learn my way round Putney.

The work I had to do was at first very simple. It consisted mainly of dealing with applications for free school lunches, helping finance school uniforms or footwear. As I fulfilled these tasks to the satisfaction of my supervisor, I was gradually given more sensitive visits to do.

I had risen in the esteem of the professional workers after I had to their amazement, and mine, dealt with a critical situation with diligence and efficiency. I had been sent to visit the home of an adolescent girl. This was to investigate the reason the mother had cancelled her daughter's school trip, after paying the deposit a few weeks earlier. My brief was to find out if some financial help was needed. But when I arrived at the tower block where the family lived, I found a mother in the throes of a psychiatric crisis. She was chasing her young daughter round the flat, brandishing a carving knife. Friday evening was not a time when I could seek help from the professional workers for the advice I needed. I dealt with the situation as best I could. It did not prove very hard to disarm this woman. She gave me the knife on my asking. After a long talk, I was able to convince her that she was at the end of her tether. She badly needed a rest from the daily stress. She readily agreed to go into hospital, once I had assured her the girls would be taken care of. By using the social contacts I had made through Noah, I was able to arrange this woman's voluntary admission to the Maudsley Hospital, even though she lived out of the catchment area. I telephoned the welfare office on the Monday morning, and reported on my visit. No one talked to me about correct procedures, nor made any negatives remarks. Thinking she may be pleased at the progress I had made in my ability to handle a difficult situation, I recounted the episode to Ms Casters. She was the only person who was rather dubious about my intervention. She declared that it had not been done by the book's rules. I did not know that there was a protocol to be used in this kind of case, and as I was not aware of it, I had managed very well without it.

Accepting that the professional workers trusted me, gave me confidence. I had not previously been conscious of the level of my ability to empathise with others, while remaining detached enough to be helpful to my interlocutors.

The work in the Subscription Department was not only very boring in itself, but the problems encountered in the job, seemed as insurmountable as trying to solve the dilemma of Sisyphus' myth. The whole set up was in such a mess that no matter how hard one tried to tidy it up, the task proved impossible. Every day my in-tray was full of letters from subscribers saying that they had not received their magazine, or got two copies addressed slightly differently. The list of complaints was endless.

The young woman responsible for the addressograph system was not very amenable to discussing queries. Her answer was always, "Put it in my in-tray".

The turnover of staff in the section was very high. Each departure of a member of staff only complicated the work of the person taking over the post. Part of the ritual of the last goodbye was the throwing away in the waste paper bin of the content of ones in-tray. Desk drawers full of queries, which had proven insoluble, met with the same fate.

This state of confusion only seemed to exist in the organisation of the medias magazines. The periodical reviews published by the firm for professional associations appeared to be managed more tidily, and the staff turnover significantly much lower. The lists of subscribers for these publications were much smaller and dealt mostly with an inland membership, while the others had a very large clientele spread all over the world. The addresses were often long and complicated, and in languages most clerks did not understand.

My mind concentrated on the demands of the social work. This made the hopelessness of the daily grind bearable, while I decided what to do next. After fifteen months of trying to push the stone up the mountain side five days a week, and two years of working for the Children's Care Office, I was ready to move.

I had tried to discuss with Ms Casters the career possibilities, which were open to me, considering my lack of qualifications. I wanted to take into account my increasing strength, and my working experience.

She thought I should try to get into the nursing profession. But I still did not feel able to cope with death too frequently, which she did not understand. I had the wholehearted support of Ms Rose at the Children's Care Office. She had really appreciated my work. So I set about contacting the Head Almoners of several London teaching hospitals. I posted a batch of letters on the Monday. Half way through Tuesday morning, a phone call from the Middlesex Hospital offered me an appointment that very day. I accepted, although I felt rather embarrassed by the informal way in which I was dressed, it being a very hot day. I wore no stockings, and had none of the formal accessories I thought I should wear for such an important occasion.

Ms Loughborough, the Head Almoner did not seem to notice my casual attire.

She had already spoken to Ms Rose, and having described the post to me, she arranged an immediate visit to the room where I would be based. This was a sub-office of the Social Work Department, and was rather unique in London. It existed to relieve the professional workers of routine tasks, which were very time consuming. It gave the almoners more time to use their specialized skills on the wards, and in outpatients department.

To my amazement quite a few of my co-workers at the magazines were upset to see me go. They had a whip round, and gave me a most magnificent Lady Ronson cigarette lighter. I had been admiring it for a long time, but it was far too expensive for me to afford. But the most precious gift, was going away having made enduring friendships, some were to last until death ended them.

The normally very discreet ritual of emptying ones in-tray and desk drawers was done for the first time, accompanied by quiet clapping mimed by my colleagues.

The management did not even bother to take leave of the staff, who was quitting the firm. The personnel officer could not get me out of his office fast enough, once he had given me the Social Security and tax documents I was to give to my next employer.

The move to the Middlesex Hospital could not have come at a better time. It offered the possibility of moving into comfortable accommodations, in the luxury staff club at a very moderate cost.

After several years of living in the Pippin's house, I had, very abruptly, been given notice to quit. Anita Pippin's mother, who owned the house, was very apologetic about it. She had no reason to advance, other than the need to give in to her daughter's demands for my swift removal. She regretfully had to comply with the latter's wish that I should go. In truth, the seeds for the crisis had been sown the instant I had walked through the door, and formed a deep bond with the little Adrian. When I started to work away from the house, the child came every morning to my room with his clothes on his arm wanting me to dress him. He was usually hanging around the hall when I came back from work, and wanted to spend time with me. When I brought a young man to the house, Adrian refused to speak to me the next day. On my enquiring about the cause of his displeasure he replied, "I don't like you because you have got a man with curly hair". The young man left.

Ms Casters seemed to be as keen to see me married as my Swiss family. She was convinced that the attachment I had with Adrian was stopping me from progressing in my relationships with men. She was right, of course, when she said that sooner or later the boy would have to accept that Anita was his mother. The sooner it happened, the better it would be for all of us. When Anita went to South America for six months with the children, it seemed that there was the chance of breaking the established pattern. On the family's return from America, Adrian tried to restart visiting early mornings with his clothes on his arm. I sent him away gently telling him that his mummy wanted to dress him. I went through the same routine in the evenings, when he turned up with his pyjamas. After a few days he gave up, but he was still spending time with me, especially at weekends. The crisis came when he caught Measles. He was feeling unwell. When his mother tried to attend to him, he sent her away, saying, "I don't want you, I want Clara to look after me". Anita could not accept that the child she had largely ignored in her years of marital unhappiness and depression, now rejected her. Her understandable solution was to get rid of the intruder. While I was packing, Adrian, now out of bed, came to see me. He asked, "If I die, will I become a baby again?" Rather brutally I answered, "I am afraid not, if you die, that is it, that is the end." When I lied in my new abode that night, I suddenly remembered the child's question. All the pent up sorrow of the day overcame me. I sobbed myself to sleep.

Finding a bedsit room in Barnes had proved very difficult, despite the numerous postcards in the newsagents' windows. It was a rather expensive borough, and the rooms I liked were too expensive for my budget. I also came across racially motivated prejudices. One landlady was all smiles until she discovered that no, I was not German but French. Her whole attitude towards me changed instantly. She suddenly discovered that she had someone else to see, which contradicted with what she had said a few minutes earlier. Another woman was blunter. She said "You are French, No men you know." Looking at the dingy room and the gas ring by the fireplace which would be my only means of cooking I replied, "I don't bring men home, but I like cooking" and pointing out the primitive facilities, I added. "So I don't think this would do."

Another woman tried to persuade me, that her house was five minutes from the bus stop. She sent her young daughter with me to prove it. The girl was running so fast, that I could not keep up with her. When I eventually caught up with the child, I took her arm, raised it in the air and declared her the winner. I then felt rather guilty, as the little girl cannot have been more than ten years old, she had only done what her mother had asked.

The last address had a Cypriot name on it, and I made my way to the house. I had at first dismissed it because it said that the room was small. However, by now I would have moved into a broom cupboard. The woman who opened the door was Liverpool born, but married to a Cypriot. She was smiling and welcoming. The cheerful, clean room was indeed small, but through a combination of good planning and taste, it had everything I may need for the moment. Even the cooking facilities were adequate to meet my demands, no oven, but two gas rings and a grill.

Before offering to take the room I asked the lady what the house restrictions were. She answered, that she did not believe in rules, as she did not want to run a miserable house. Within a few hours, I was installed in the little nest. I was to stay there seven happy months. During the spring and summer, I spent a lot of my free time walking on the common. I often sat near the pond where I had so often taken

Adrian to feed the ducks. But I never saw him, and gradually I lost hope.

When the cold weather came, I could not spend time outside. The exiguity of my accommodation began to weigh on me. My claustrophobia was accentuated by the position of the window. It was set so high, that I could only look out by standing on a chair. But if the offer of accommodation at the Middlesex staff club had not been forthcoming, I would have found ways of coping. I enjoyed staying in this quietly friendly house, after the histrionics of the family I had just left.

The move to the staff club, offered among other advantages the chance of living in central London. It was situated in Lancaster Gate, one side of it facing Hyde Park. It took me fifteen minute to travel to work, instead of the hour I had to allow from Barnes. The club retained many features of the good class hotel it had once been. The rooms were well furnished, each one even had its own telephone linked to the club's main switchboard. Uniformed porters and reception staff were always on duty. Main meals were served at the table, and hot beverages could be ordered at other times. The substantial reduction in my daily travelling expenses and the small increase in salary I was now being paid, made it possible for me to live at the club. I also enjoyed going to the theatre most weeks, sitting in the gods for half a crown, or a few shillings in the back breaking back row of Covent Garden. The most expensive ticket I ever bought, cost me seven shillings and six pence. This was a Christmas performance of the Nutcracker Suite, my very first visit to the ballet.

My duties at the hospital made me feel that for the very first time ever, I was doing work that mattered to others. Whether I was going round the wards, helping patients to keep up to date with their medical certificates, or sitting in the office paying out to patients the cost of their fare. I learned to assess their rights to have surgical appliances subsidized by the National Health Service, or how to trace misled case notes. We were four clerks in the office, and each one of us could do any part of the work, while having a well-defined area of responsibility. My special job was finding and filing the Social workers case notes. The senior of our little office, Ms Garvey, a strict but very fair woman, soon boasted that I could put my hands on a set of notes in less than 3 minutes. Out of over 30.000 folders that was quite a record. The greatest compliment ever paid to me by the senior clerk Ms Garvey, was once that I had acknowledged having made a mistake, she said, "That is not like you, you are always so careful."

For the first time in my working life, I did not feel in danger of losing my employment. The rules of the hospital were clear and well defined, respecting them was all that was required for safety. I no longer felt dependent on the caprices or moods of a boss, or an intolerant relative. Very quickly, I lost the nagging anxiety, which had plagued my life for so long. For the first time since I had left the orphanage, it being the only other place where I never felt in danger of being thrown out, I felt safe. My mother had so often made this threat to me, giving me a childhood of uncertainty. This anguish had been compounded in adolescence, by my family's ambivalence towards me.

Ms Casters had not been very pleased, when I had applied for a post in top teaching hospitals. She kept telling me that I would stand a better chance in more modest establishments. Guided by Ms Rose, who had appreciated my work at the Children's Care Office, I had ignored the advice of the social worker, and was glad that I had. But this had damaged further our already fraught relationship. I thought that she had a really poor opinion of me. She felt sure that only second-rate establishments would consider employing me. It was some months later, that I discovered her objections to my working at the Middlesex, had a more personal and understandable reason.

The filing system of the department was getting clogged up. Ms Garvey asked me to go through all the records, and pack for incineration social notes of patients who had not been seen by an almoner for a period of ten years or more. I was to exclude from this clear out children, the elderly and severely handicapped people who may need help again.

Little Mau, the youngest clerk in the office, offered to help me when she could. I started with the Letter A, and my colleague at the other end of the alphabet.

It was not long before I got to the letter C, and quite accidentally came across Ms Casters' case notes. She had attended the hospital as an in-patient some years before to undergo major surgery. During her hospitalization, she had used the moral support of the relevant Almoner. She had corresponded with her for a while after her discharge. I was very disturbed by my discovery, as I realized that I had attributed unworthy motifs to the woman. I was suddenly in a state of acute terror, in case she was going to die. I also did not know what to do with this unwelcome knowledge. I was sure I could not face her again while carrying this secret. So I did what I always did when I had something important to impart to her, I wrote a letter. The reply, by return of post told me that there was nothing for me to worry about. She had not had any kind of malignancy, and she was perfectly all right. The more complex causes of my distress were not discussed further. The matter was never to be referred to again. When I was beyond the phase of thinking only about my side of the upset, I was able to appreciate how awful it must have been for Ms Casters to have her most intimate privacy so invaded. But it took a while for me to get there.

Chapter Twenty-Two

Soon after that Ms Casters told me that she was leaving her post, as family demands necessitated that she worked nearer home. She was returning to work in the psychiatric hospital, where she had started her career. I was very upset at the thought of losing her. Despite our frequent squabbles, she was the wall on which I had been leaning for some years. True, not a smooth comfortable wall, but a solid dependable one. She suggested keeping in touch, but I did not quite believe she meant it and told her so. She then said to me in a tone, which seemed to be full of sadness. "You really have very little idea of what you get from people". The sentence stuck in my head, even if I was unable to appreciate the full meaning of it. I felt that it a reproach, I must somehow deserve.

When I visited her at Worthfield, I found a much more relaxed Ms Casters. She was almost friendly. She had worked at the hospital during the war serving the needs of the psychiatric patients during the day, and helping in the military canteen in the evenings. Huge prefabricated wards lodged the military personnel. This contrasted dramatically with the well-built facilities, which housed the mental patients. After the war, the military facilities had been taken over by the psychiatric services. In them were accommodated the expanding mentally ill population. I was pleased that the conversation was for once diverted from me, but of course, it could not last. Eventually, she asked how things were going with the young man I had been seeing for a while. I knew for a long time, that she wanted to see me married. She was probably seeing in the marital state a chance for me to have at last the stability of family life. But I would not, or more precisely I could not oblige. I was never short of suitors, but all the courtships ended in disaster. Everything went well until the young man became too serious, and demanded some commitment on my part. I was then overtaken by a panic that sometimes amounted to terror. All of a sudden the very agreeable boy friend was transformed into a monster. When this happened I had only one thought in mind, "Get rid of him". I was never enjoying the end of the romance. I was in a state of acute anxiety, which caused me to loose several pounds in weight in a few days. When the whole episode was finally over, I had an overwhelming feeling of relief, now I could relax.

Because of the milieu in which I moved, all the young men I met were professional, well-educated fellows. Each one of them would have been in the eyes of Ms Casters a very desirable candidate for matrimony. Thus I worked my way through a few doctors, a couple of teachers, a young Indian millionaire and a social worker. I was now enjoying the company of the Personnel Officer of a large industrial firm. All was going well, and I was even considering breaking my strict rules; giving him my all, and enjoy a pleasant string-free liaison. At that moment the young man, whose name was Eliot announced that the time had come for me to meet his parents. We should put our relationship on a formal footing. I took it that by this he meant we should soon get engaged to be married. I said laughingly, "Plenty of time for commitment, you do not have to feel rushed." I was trying to slow things down, putting off the unavoidable ghastly moment of the break up. However, the next time I saw him, he had already arranged for us both to have lunch at his parents home the following Sunday.

Saturday I developed a severe migraine, and was confined to a dark room. I vomited anything I tried to ingest. I was in severe pain, and had to cancel the appointment with Eliot's family. I was ill the whole weekend and could not face work at the start of the week. Towards the end of Tuesday, I was feeling considerably better, and planned to go back to work the following day. During the evening, the young man telephoned me. He announced that his parents would be pleased to receive us the following Sunday.

Within a few hours, I had severely relapsed. The pain was so bad, that I felt like hitting my head on the wall. I consulted my general practitioner the following morning. Dr. Thomas, on hearing the story of my symptoms said to me, "I will give you a prescription to treat the migraine, but the most useful treatment would be for you to go home and sort out your life." I was very impressed that she had not pried and I had not confided in her. I instantly decided that I was not going to meet Eliot ever again. Before the end of the day I had I recovered. The next day I went back to work.

I typed Eliot a two-line note brutally saying that I did not want to see him again. I gave no reason. I did not have any that I could mention. During my lunch hour, I went to the mews house at the back of Harley Street which he shared with a couple of friends, and put the note in his letter box. I went back to work totally unconcerned. Little Mo suggested that it might not be a good idea to go back to the Club immediately after work. I really could not see a reason not to. I was sure he was not going to come looking for me. Why should he? Almost all of my previous boy friends had taken their dismissal quietly. All I could think about was how relieved I felt to have him off my back. After all it was his fault, he had pressurised me into wedlock. I did, however, give in to the entreaties of Little Mo, and agreed to stay out of the way for the evening. We went to see the musical Oliver, which we had promised ourselves to do for some time.

When I returned to the Club, the receptionist was in a state of effervescence. Eliot had been there the whole evening. I had missed him by minutes. He had written me countless letters, which he threw in the waste paper basket. I apologised profusely. The Staff was very forgiving. I needed their help and support during the following weeks. Every day Eliot subjected me to two of three things: letters, phone calls, numerous bunches of flowers. It looked as if it would never end. I spoke to the very friendly hospital security officers. They said that unless I was physically threatened, there was nothing they could do. One evening, as I came out of the hospital with Little Mo, Eliot appeared apparently out of nowhere, and grabbed me. He was only asking me to go to a café and have a talk, but I was very frightened. With my friend's help, I managed to free myself. Then it was all hell let loose. The hospital security officers became involved, as well as the police on Goodge street. When I told them where Eliot lived, and what his job was, there was a sudden reluctance on the part of the officers to be too direct in their approach. They asked me if we had friends in common. I mentioned the name of the politician who had introduced us. The suggestion from the police was that I should get him to speak to Eliot. Aaron was in the middle of an election campaign, in which he was a candidate. But he dropped everything to speak to Eliot and calm him down, which he succeeded in doing. He told me later that he had even shown him some sympathy, when Eliot had said that I had spurned his love and broken his heart. But Aaron's wife knew Eliot of old, as she too had had trouble with him. He had pursued her, and been very nasty about Aaron's premature baldness and his ethnicity, when the pair became engaged to be married.

Eliot promised Aaron that he would leave me alone. In view of the proportions the incident had taken, I too had to give the police my word that I would follow their instructions. I was told to leave London for a week, and not tell anyone where I would be. On my return to work, I was to leave the hospital every day through a different exit, changing the pattern weekly until I was satisfied that all was well. Luckily, the hospital has a number of underground passages and exits, which made it easy for me to comply with the police recommendations.

Ms Keane, the Club administrator was going to the Lake District for a week, and she suggested I accompany her. Her kindness was not rewarded as deserved. I was in what the French called, "un etat second", and not very communicative. Luckily, she was a very chatty woman, and I hoped she enjoyed being listened to for a change. She did spend her working life, listening to her staff and some very demanding residents. The whole week, I just went along with whatever she suggested. On our return she told her secretary what an easy person I was to have around.

This last relationship fiasco had given me a serious jolt. I was now nearly 28 years old, and my life seemed to be in a cul de sac. I had to accept that I did not seem able to get married. It was not so much that I did not want to, but that I could not. I could not fully understand what was wrong. I knew I had a fear of becoming dependent, and loose the ability to stand on my own two feet. It had been so hard learning to cope on my own. I could not trust anyone not to leave me, or die on me. Being let down by people had been after all my life's experience, be it by rejection or by death. I had always ended up alone, and I had learned to rely only on myself. The job at the Hospital was a very comfortable little nest, and I was beginning to worry about it. I feared it might be softening me up. I knew that if I stayed there, I would be a clerk for the rest of my working life. I had to make a move while I still could. But I had no qualifications of any sort, and with only experience I would not go very far or ever feel totally secure.

When I had been working at the Middlesex for a while, some of the Almoners encouraged me to train as a social worker. I had applied to London University for a place on a course. Now that I was over 25 I qualified as a mature student, for whom success in an entrance examination could secure me a place. I passed this test and was lucky to be interviewed by a sympathetic panel. However, the Borough refused me a grant, saying I had not been resident there long enough. The following year I was spontaneously offered a grant, so I applied again for a university place. The interviewers were very aggressive. I lost my composure, wrecking my chances of getting a place.

By chance I met a mental welfare officer, who told me that another way of getting in the profession was by the bias of a psychiatric nursing qualification. This is what he had done, he declared himself very happy with his status. I had by now been to Worthfield several times, and decided to apply for training there. To pacify Ms Casters, I had taken the precaution of going to the Royal College of Nursing to ask a list of recommended psychiatric nursing schools in the London area. The woman I saw gave me the information I required, after spending in vain some minutes trying to put me off this branch of the profession.

I wrote to Ms Casters informing her of my intentions to train as a psychiatric nurse. I gave her a list of the hospitals I had applied to including Worthfield. The only thing I did not tell her was that I had sent the letter to that hospital a few days before I posted the others.

She understood that I was determined to get on with my plans. Having failed to persuade me that the work would be too hard for me, she arranged for one of the French nurses to show me the wards. I had to admit to myself that the psycho-geriatric units were a tough prospect. But the disturbed wards did not put me off, and there were a number of admission wards where I could well see myself working. Anyway, it was a means to an end, and for the first time I had the chance of having a formal training leading to a recognised qualification. As I hoped, the matron from Worthfield was the first one to reply to my letter and offer me an interview.

The interview had almost been too easy. I had expected to have to sell myself, but it was the Matron, who did her best to sell the hospital to me. She knew that on a previous visit, I had done a thorough tour of the women's side of this large psychiatric hospital. I had seen the very best and the worst wards. I had not been put off the idea of psychiatric nursing by seeing the psycho-geriatric units, any more than I had been on going round the airy and more comfortable admission's wards.

My motivation for wanting to come to Worthfield was a mixture of conflicting elements but my determination was rock solid. I went back to London with the verbal offer of a place on the next introductory course, and waited impatiently for the written confirmation.

When the letter arrived, I went into shock realising the enormity of what I had done. For several days, I was hardly able to function, so horrified was I at the thought of the plunge I was about to make. I was giving up a secure post in the Almoners' department of one of the most prestigious London Teaching Hospitals. The post held no promotional prospect, but due to my apparent fragility, I was treated with a kindness I had never known anywhere before. I was aware that this attitude was not due solely to the fact that I did my job well, so did everyone else. It was all so cosy but dangerously mollifying. It was partly due to the over solicitude of the social work staff that after two years working in this very caring environment, I had decided it was time to move on while I still could. I was scared that if I stayed, my ability to stand on my own two feet would be eroded. So now, I was embarking on a course of study for one of the most demonised professions there was in the health service, certainly one of the most despised.

The reaction of my superiors did nothing to allay my anguish. The dapper little Brigadier who was Hospital Secretary called me for a final interview. He warned me, that I would not meet nice people in a mental hospital. Some years later, I heard that he had become Master of a royal household. I thought maybe someone should have given him the same warning, when he went to work at the palace.

By the time I had worked my month's notice, I recovered my spirits. I was given a most generous send off, and the assurance that a post would always be there for me should I wish to return.

PART THREE

LOOKING AT THE STARS

Chapter Twenty-Three

Nothing had prepared me for the culture shock, which awaited me on my arrival at the nurses' home of Worthfield Hospital. The reception offered to the new girls was abrupt. We were herded in the home sister's small office. When she gave me instructions by addressing herself to "Nurse!" without adding my name to it, I did not, at first, realise that she was talking to me. When at last I heard her, I felt like shouting that it was all a mistake. I was not a nurse but a fraud. I was here under false pretences. Could I please leave now? If the friend who had given me a lift to the hospital had not already gone, I may at that instant have turned on my heels. But there I was, stuck in the middle of the country with all my worldly goods in one large trunk and a couple of battered suitcases. With no means of transport, and in any case no home to go to, I had to stay.

I soon found myself in the tiny room, which was to be my home. The accommodation was rudimentary, even by the standards of the day. A metal bed, one small armchair, what seemed to be a child's wardrobe, a dressing table and a hand basin completed my living quarters. Lavatories and bathrooms were, of course, communal, the latter being very generous propagators of the athlete's foot mushrooms.

On each floor a tiny kitchenette was available for nurses' use. It served about 50 rooms. It was monopolised by the nurses from the

Iberian peninsula. They seemed to dislike the food served in the huge, noisy dining room. On that first evening, I decided that the food was not so much served as thrown at you. Not a very cheering experience.

The next morning the new students were to assemble in the home sisters office at 8 am. Some of the girls had worked at the hospital as nursing assistants. They knew the geography of the place. To them fell the task of guiding the newcomers to the school of nursing, and to the linen room to be kitted out with uniforms. The old hands in our group were a mixture of West Indians, Portuguese and Irish girls. The Benjamin of the class, Sarah, was the only English student among us. She was also, as it turned out, the troublemaker of the group. The old hands very much enjoyed lording it over the newcomers. Completely lost in this enormous hospital, we allowed ourselves to be patronized, having no choice in the matter.

Worthfield had been built in 1930. Its layout differed very much from the classical Victorian lunatic asylum of the 19th century. The hospital was not surrounded by high walls. Trees, hedges and bushes formed its borders, more in the manner of the English country estate, which it once was. The buildings resembled those of a large housing estate, as these were planned before the era of the tower blocks. The one aspect, which helped to differentiate it from a council development, was the impression it gave of having been built in a beautiful country park. The numerous trees, lawns, shrubs and flowerbeds were all beautifully maintained. The beauty of the surroundings had been one of the attractions to me.

The old mansion still dominated the landscape. In it was accommodated the school of nursing, and some junior medical staff. Consultants, who lived within the grounds of the hospital, were afforded a comfortable detached house.

We had no male students in our class. This rendered the invisible frontier separating the men's side of the hospital from the women's wards, almost palpable. The female side was further divided into two divisions, each with its own set of administrative, medical and nursing staff. Each area had its own ethos, philosophy and atmosphere. It reminded me of the way each Swiss canton, seems to be in a different country than its nearest neighbour.

During these first few weeks, the cultural variants of the hospital did not concern me overmuch. The physical discomforts of my living quarters, which were really Spartan, depressed me. I felt rather isolated, as the nurses seemed to move in the very restricted circles of their nationality or affinity. I did not seem able to fit in any of the existing group. There were a number of French nurses, but most of them were still at the stage of running down everything British. This collided fiercely with the uncritical love affair I had been enjoying with the country for some years. Other more profound differences were to appear, which were to have a most deleterious effect on my weak capacity to fit in this alien world. Almost from the day of my arrival in Worthfield, the pattern of the next few years took shape. I was to be a resounding professional success, but a dismal social failure.

In this disaster, were included my relationship with my classmates. They very quickly took a violent dislike to anything I appear to represent. They called me a swot and a snob. I was 10 years older than the youngest student on the course. I was too keen to prove not only to myself, but to the teaching staff, that I was up to doing the academic work. I tried hard to shine in practical demonstrations. This was easier than it seemed. The girls who had worked as nursing assistant had acquired bad professional habits. The nurse tutors were working patiently to eradicate these corner-cutting practices. By application and some luck, I nearly always got top marks, for my work both written and practical. This engendered some quite vicious jealousy. Childish graffiti appeared on classroom blackboards. Some accused me of having a crush on one of the male tutors. I responded in the worst possible way, letting the class know that I thought they were a pathetic bunch. I was sent to Coventry by the whole class. I survived on the respect and esteem shown to me by the school staff. Understandably, the tutors' attitude towards me aggravated the hostility of my classmates.

The leader of my tormentors was Sarah, the youngest student in the group. Nothing I could have done, justified the relentless persecution, which I had to endure. I decided that if she hated me for what I was, rather than for anything I may have done, I could do nothing about it. After some weeks, I discovered that she was having a feud with the entire French contingent. This was due to an incident, which had taken place before I arrived at the hospital.

Sarah was accused of having seduced the Irish fiancé of one of the French nurses, after a rather boozy party. Sarah's Irish fiancé, known to be a violent man gave the guilty pair a severe beating. After which he forgave Sarah, and fixed a wedding date. It says a great deal about the level of Sarah's maturity that she blamed Camille, the wronged woman, for the beating she had received. She decided to marry Paddy, by whom she was already pregnant, and in doing so signed a contract on a life of battering.

Some of the West Indians in the class had worked at the hospital as nursing assistants. They acted as guides and mentors to the newcomers. Together they formed a very tight little group. I had always had a rather sentimental attitude towards the blacks, which I saw as downtrodden and ill used. I was not prepared for this noisy, exuberant bunch of girls. They talked loudly, laughed louder and their belches had the sound of trumpet calls. The belches annoyed and disgusted me. At the mid morning break the hospital gave us a generous helping of coffee, bread, butter and jam. One of the West Indians girls Daisy on finishing her food had the habit of putting one hand on her stomach, and letting out a thunderous belch. One day, I felt so irritated that I decided to tell her so. I said to her. "You know, this is not done" to which she asked, "What do you mean. Do you mean this is not done?" I replied, "This is not done in society". Unbeaten she pursued. "In what kind of society?" I said coldly. "In civilised society". She was silenced. The following day she let out one last trumpeting belch, but never did it again in my presence.

This incident, which should have increased the dislike of the group towards me, seemed to have had the opposite effect. In the absence of Sarah, the West Indians students began to speak to me. On Friday evenings, I met them on the coach when we escaped to London for the weekend. They asked my help in orientating themselves in the maze of the capital's underground trains. We also had hilarious moments in shops, where I helped them find affordable warm clothing.

On Monday mornings as soon as Sarah appeared, I returned to Coventry. I knew by then, that very soon my enemy would be going on maternity leave. She would be lost to the group. When she resumed her duties, she would be put back one class. This knowledge helped me cope with the on going tensions.

On our first day in the school of nursing, we had met the principal tutor, Reggy Loader. He was an attractive man in his forties. He could have had a truly handsome face, if it had not been soiled by an almost permanently worried look. His little blond moustache, slanted downwards on the sides of his mouth. One soon realised that it was not the moustache that drooped, but his face. It had the signs that the man to whom it belonged, had given up hope of ever getting to the top of the mountain. But he could not, nevertheless, stop himself from trying to get there.

In our first meeting with Reggy, he informed us that Worthfield Hospital existed, and was run mainly for the benefit of the staff. The needs of the patients came poorly second to the comfort and wellbeing of the salaried personnel. Any measures introduced, or even suggested for the improvement of the care given to patients, did not stand a chance of succeeding if it interfered with the "joie de vivre" of the staff, their convenience and general ease. It was a theme the principal was to return to many times in the three years I was to spend under his tutorship.

Another of his favourite complaints was the undue importance given to the occupational therapists, whom he referred to as "the green bitches". Their dark green uniforms were indeed to be seen all over the hospital. Although they were outnumbered by the nurses several hundred to one, they gave themselves airs of importance. This grated on our Reggy's nerves, and on quite a few of the nurses. Many had to spend several hours daily in their company. Most of the O.Ts were middle class girls. Their poise and self-confidence irritated the more modest nursing staff. We were encouraged by our tutor to make the life of these snooty pieces as awkward as possible. The students in my class, who had already encountered the green beasties, were only too keen to concur with this view. Being new in the hospital, I had no experience of the species, but I was rather disturbed by this reversal of status. At the Middlesex Hospital, the nurses were considered to be little princesses by the rest of the personnel. Each ward Sister was indeed the queen of her domain. All other staff were schooled on entering the hospital into believing that the nurses were the most important persons in the institution after the patients. We were warned by the Brigadier never to keep a nurse waiting. Nurses were part of the vital system, which kept the hospital alive and the patients safe. I had indeed entered another world.

Ms Boyle the only woman tutor was a very proper spinster. She taught practical nursing, anatomy and physiology. If there were male students in the class, they were sent out while the tutor instructed the girls in the detail of their reproductive system. The male tutor Davee Thomas, instructed the boys into the mysteries of their genital functioning. We had no boys in our class, and so were deprived of this piece of obsolete educational ballet. Judging from the conversation my fellow students enjoyed during coffee breaks, most of them could have taught gentle Ms Boyle a few things about male physiology.

Towards the end of the introductory course, an SOS was sent to the school from women's admission wards. This was transmitted to us by Reggy Loaner. A volunteer was needed after 5pm to look after a woman who required second by second supervision. On hearing the name of the patient, a certain Mrs F., none of the students came forwards. I was very keen to go to the ward, but I had as yet no practical experience and said so.

Reggy retorted that I had to start sometime, so why not now? The ward sister, who was none other than his wife, would explain clearly what was expected of me. When the class ended, I set off to the ward followed by the sarcastic good wishes of my classmates.

Sister Paula Loaner was a short, tubby woman in her forties. Her blond hair was cut in an unfashionable sporty style. She was not just bustly. She bustled all over. She was excellent at her job. I was to find out later that she was also a most dreadful gossip. However, on my first evening on the ward, I found her a first class instructor. After a very short but clear briefing Sister L introduced me to Mrs F. My task was simple enough: I was not for a single instant to take my eyes off the patient, even if it meant sneezing in her face! She was a most unpredictable woman, who was liable to make a self destructive move at any moment. If I needed to absent myself even briefly I was to call a nurse, then wait until someone was available to take over until I returned. The next four hours were to be the most important lesson in observation I was ever to receive.

Mrs F. was a woman in her forties who had been a psychiatric social worker before her marriage. Her husband was a well-respected psychoanalyst. The couple had several children. Mrs F. had been in analysis with a doctor who had the misfortune to drown in a Scottish loch. The accident, which had taken place during a psychoanalytic congress, had cost the lives of several analysts.

Mrs F. had taken the loss of her analyst very hard. The poor woman had gone totally to pieces. She had made several attempts on her life. The last one had been when she had succeeded in throwing herself out of an upstairs window in a psychiatric unit. She had sustained multiple fractures, and was now walking awkwardly.

In those days the wards still had open fires in the observation dormitories, where the most disturbed patients spent their days. I barely had the time to take my environment in, when the action starts: Mrs F. gets up from her chair. I get up from my seat next to hers. Mrs F. does a semi-circle and attempts to sit in the lit fireplace. I grab her in my arms and she sits back in her armchair without too much protest. She then asks me for a cigarette, which I light for her as instructed. While she smokes my hands are poised to thwart her efforts at stubbing it out on her throat. Half way through the cigarette, I get a little tired of the game. I take it away and throw it in the fireplace. Mrs F. looks at me, and laughs. I laugh with her. We are friends for life. She will always be Bertie for me, and I will always be "the smart one" for her.

After four exhausting hours I leave the ward feeling that I am now on my way to be a psychiatric nurse. Sister L appreciates me. She will call on me again to look after Bertie, or stand vigil in the observation dormitory. I am glad to have found this interesting niche to do overtime, where I can satisfy my dual needs of learning and earning.

Chapter Twenty-Four

At the end of the six weeks introductory course, the whole class was in effervescence. In which ward where we to get our first experience as student nurses? On our last day in school, the ward allocation sheet was pinned on the notice board of the nurses home. We all ran there in excited anticipation. My heart sank, when I saw that my first posting was to be a ward for seriously deteriorated senile women. I had hoped to be allocated to the admission ward, a foolish wish for a total beginner.

I tried to find out as much as possible about FG1. The ward was home for 48 old ladies in advanced state of senility. The staff consisted of a sister on each shift, a solitary student nurse, and a handful of nursing assistants, mostly Hispanic. A long-stay patient came in daily from another ward to do the heavy cleaning.

I was warded on Sister Eva Kramer's shift. A very young German woman, described as very strict but fair. Meeting her was quite an experience. She was certainly under thirty years old, and did not fit the image one had of a ward Sister. She was of medium height, fair with a boyish haircut. Her almost totally flat figure, gave her the appearance of a rather good-looking adolescent Aryan boy.

On my first morning her welcoming words were "Good morning nurse, so you are to be my only student nurse, tough on you and tough on me." I took it that the remark referred to my lack of experience, and was in no way personally derogatory. It was still a rather cold reception, which took sometimes to get over. She ran the ward efficiently, but tolerated nursing assistants, who occasionally cut corners, and to whom she referred to as, "the lesser endowed". As far as the students were concerned, she insisted on perfection at all time. It was a very good training, but it was hard. I felt sandwiched between a boss, who tolerated nothing but the best, and outnumbered by rarely friendly auxiliaries who demanded speed above all.

Nursing assistants often enjoyed making the life of students miserable. These women had failed to train due to language problems or lack of academic ability. Their jealousy was quite understandable. The pettiness of their behaviour was less so. On my first morning on the ward, the answer to my query as to the location of the staff lavatories was "you have been to the school you should know". I said calmly, "don't worry, I will just ask Sister", which prompted a lot of curses in Spanish, accompanied by the direction I needed.

After some weeks of continual obstruction from the Spanish contingent, I had a stroke of luck. A well-educated, delightful Portuguese girl joined the ward team. Preciosa had been around for sometime. A fluent French speaker, she was very friendly towards me. This was an added bonus, as it eased my isolation on the ward. As soon as the other Hispanic girls started to speak in their mother tongue, we broke into French, which had the effect of silencing the others. Preciosa was pursuing a part-time academic course in London. She paid her way, by working as a nursing assistant.

We had to make sure Sister did not catch us speaking in a tongue other than English. She rightly pointed out, that speaking a foreign language in a ward of profoundly senile patients, only added to their confusion. Most of the old ladies were totally disorientated in time and space. The work was of the most unglamorous kind, and physically extremely exhausting. A great many patients were paralysed. They had to be lifted in and out of bed, chair and lavatory. The incontinent ones, had to be washed and changed throughout the day and at night.

Some of them had degraded personal habits such as putting their fingers in their anal cavity. They ended up with faeces drying up under their nails. A few were seated in restraining chairs. These seats, not unlike an adult version of babies' high chairs, prevented the women from falling and sustaining fractures.

The noise in the ward was deafening. Certain patients shouted endlessly, others repeated the same sentence during their waking hours. A very gentle lady told us all day that "Dr. Lucas said, every little helps". A relative of a celebrated war heroine ran around the ward asking "Where is the baby? Under the bed? under the birdie?". One day she went into the dormitory just as the floor had been washed, slipped, broke her femur, developed a chest infection and died.

One old lady was in the habit of resisting any attempt to wash and dress her. The task of getting her ready for the day was further complicated by our need to keep ourselves away from her saliva. She accumulated it in her mouth until the supply was adequate to spit in our faces. The first time I was detailed to care for her, I saw a concentration camp number tattooed on her arm. I wondered what vengeance she thought she was assuaging in this way. She had totally lost the power of speech, as had so many of our residents. Some could be comforted, but this one could not bear to have anyone touch her. I felt helpless and rather sad. I could do so little for her.

One day I was transferring a lady from her bed to a wheelchair on my own. We often had to do these things unaided, due to the shortage of staff. The patient, not normally aggressive, must have feared that I was going to let her fall on the floor. She tried to save herself from this none existent danger, by grabbing my breast and would not let it go. Even when installed in the wheelchair, she held on. The pain was excruciating, I thought I was going to faint. I managed to free myself, while making reassuring noises to make her feel safe. When she had let go of me, I had beads of perspiration running down my face. I knew she had not meant to be aggressive. She was just frightened.

Some of these senile women were violent. They could inflict quite serious injuries to nurses. Whether out of malice or fear, these apparently fragile old things could do us a lot of damage. The Hispanic nurse assistants varied a great deal in their capacity to tolerate aggression. It was hard for all of us to differentiate between deliberate attacks, and hurting gestures born out of fear. I suspected certain nurses of retaliating when they were hurt. I added to my unpopularity, by my apparent acceptance of blows. The nickname of "OLD FLO" was soon mine. It irritated me to be compared to Florence Nightingale in this way, but I never let it be known. I knew only too well that to show signs of impatience would ensure that I would never be called by any other name.

The ward was rather a long way from the nurses' homes. One could also make a dash across the grass. I often used this quicker method in the morning, to avoid being late. Looking at my wet shoes covered in green mowings, Sister Kramer said one day, "I see you belong to the walking across the grass brigade." I took it that she meant I was going to be a source of trouble for her. I redoubled my efforts towards perfection. This trying very hard to please Sister Kramer had to be tempered with a somewhat neutral facial expression, so as not to give the wrong message. She had the reputation of being a very seductive lesbian. She always behaved with the most perfect professionalism towards me. Maybe I was not just her type of girl. She was really rather beautiful, in a very cold sort of way. Her very pale face never showed the slightest trace of make up. Her fair hair, cut in a boyish style, accentuated her androgynous look. One could not say that she looked masculine. She was far too delicate. She had more the look of an adolescent Scandinavian prince.

She appeared to take great pleasure, in making men look foolish and inadequate. The ward doctor was a tall gentle fellow. She treated him in a rather malicious manner, and seemed to enjoy humiliating. She did so by demanding that he performed impossible tasks, and sniggered when he failed. Dr. Waver endeared himself to me by his patience, and apparent lack of resentment at this rather shameful treatment. I was all admiration.

Behind Sister's back, I used my eyes to flirt with him. To my surprise he responded to my message. It would have been a very bad idea to give my senior the slightest hint that a budding romance was taking place under her very nose. Positive action had to be delayed until a more propitious time. At that precise moment, she was busy bullying Dr. Waver into attempting to cure manually a double prolapse on the person of a very senile woman in her eighties. As soon as the poor man had succeeded in returning the uterus to its proper place, the rectum, which he had replaced earlier, came out again. Beads of perspiration were rolling down from his forehead, to the tip of his nose. Sister Kramer scoffed at his inability to perform a miracle, proving to her yet again, as if necessary, the uselessness of all men. To add to the poor patient's misery, her tongue, which was very large, was also protruding. In her discomfort she made the most horrendous noise. My task was to hold her in the required position to assist this useless procedure. I tried to calm her understandable anguish. Sister's great moment of glory came when the wretched medical man had to admit defeat. While he wrote a few words on the patient's case notes, General K marched off to her office with the triumphant air that Wellington must have had after Waterloo. I fell in love with the defeated Napoleon.

Sister Kramer exerted a fascination on all who approached her. Was it her beauty, her very coldness, her great ability and intelligence or even the unkind streak some detected in her? Personally, I appreciated the utter professionalism with which she ran the ward, but above all her dry wit. I knew, that among all the women of her sexual persuasion at Worthfield, she would have been the one I could have been seduced by, had I been so inclined. She probably would have given me hell, as the gossip said she gave to all her conquests. But luckily for me, my needs were elsewhere.

In the closed world of the mental hospital this was soon known. One morning, on Sister Kramer's day off, I met her, the quite different, Sister Wiggings. She greeted me with, "so you are Nurse Cobin. I hear you are the only French girl here who does not sing, 'thank heaven for little girls'"! I understood immediately what she meant, although her remark was somewhat exaggerated. There were a few heterosexual French nurses at Worthfield, but not many. Most of the straight ones were middle-aged ward sisters. The gay girls formed a younger group.

When I first arrived at the hospital, I could not believe all that was said about the sexual proclivity of my compatriots. This was partly because I had never been part of a clique. I did not understand how such groups functioned. But I had reached the age of twenty-eight, and had not lived what could be remotely called a sheltered life. My eyes should have opened a little wider. I had known very few gay women, and every time, the discovery had been a genuine surprise. I had worked for nearly two years at the Middlesex Hospital with a woman who referred to her living companion as "her better half", or as Alex, whom I understood to be a man. That is, until the person in question came into the office. I was introduced to a woman called Alexandra, who would not have been out of place in a rugby team. I hid my surprise well, but in the present context I was to pay dearly for my crass ineptitude in handling my gay compatriots.

Trying to ease my feelings of isolation, I invited all the French girls for drinks in my room, without any discrimination of sexual orientation. Men were not allowed in the nurses' home, so the few heterosexual nurses came alone. The gay girls arrived with their love interest of the moment. Most of my visitors were senior students, but two ward sisters turned up. The French, Pauline Lebrec, arrived with Sister Kramer whom I had also invited.

The little party started well enough, but by the time the girls had had rather a lot to drink, they had discovered my hatbox. This had the effect of producing great hilarity. Dainty feminine hats propped on cropped heads looked very ridiculous. I tried hard to join in the general merriment. Pauline Lebrec took the opportunity of the distraction caused by the discovery of the hats, to make a rather crude pass at me. I ignored her offer, but she persisted. When Eva Kramer saw my predicament, she got me out of the difficulty. She told her friend to go and play elsewhere, which she did. As the party was beginning to show signs of degradation, I very clumsily threw them all out. They were never to forgive my rejection. I too would never forgive myself. For want of a good dose of humour, and a little tact, I had turned a group of women who were all my seniors against me. I had a lot to learn, and the learning was going to be long and painful.

What was so amazing about Sister Kramer was her apparent lack of resentment towards me, after the party. I had not slept all night, so scared was I of the repercussion my rashness may have brought on my head. She did not make the slightest allusion to the party, and went on treating with the same professionalism she had always done. At the end of my stay on the ward, she gave me an excellent report. She told me in confidence that she would be leaving soon to pursue advanced studies at London University. She advised me not to let the grass grow under my feet, once I passed my exams. I thought this advice a little premature. I still had almost all of my training to go through. But I felt that coming from such a reserved person, it was certainly the nearest she could come to paying a professional compliment.

Her parting shot was a reminder of something she had told me on one of the rare occasions we had had a private conversation. I had told her that I found Worthfield an unusually gossipy place. Having come from a very benevolent hospital, it had been a shock to me. She had said, "You will be all right, if you remember that in this hospital if you speak to a man, they say you are a prostitute, if you speak to a woman, they say you are a lesbian, but if you do not speak to anyone, they will say you do it all yourself! So study hard, do your work and always refuse to discuss your private life with anyone. It will not stop them from talking, but at least you will not put fuel on their fire. Let them burn their own fingers, putting coal on the embers".

After my little party I became the "bête noire" of the French girls and their friends. I was the victim of a relentless persecution. I could not even go to have a bath without locking my bedroom door. This was the only way, I could be sure of finding the room intact on my return. When I forgot do so, my ornaments would be broken, my books defaced and occasionally some object would be missing. I knew that complaining to the home sister would only make matters worse, that is if I was believed. The French contingent had the reputation of being a very cohesive group, irrespective of sexual orientation. My relationship problems would have been quite rightly laid at my door. In any event, the material loss I suffered was nothing compared to the unpleasant atmosphere in which I had to live.

I was told that Pauline Lebrec boasted of planning to make my life hell, should I ever be warded under her authority. But pure luck, or most probably the wisdom of the Deputy Matron, saved me from having to face this ordeal. As I was learning how the nursing administration functioned, I thought this was probably my reward for keeping my problems to myself. However, it was always in fear and trembling that I approached the notice board when the nurses' allocation was displayed.

Towards the end of my first year, I was allocated to the epileptic ward. I was to have my first experience of a thoroughly institutionalised ward sister. Sister Randall was not many years off her retirement date. She had been in charge of the same ward too long. She seemed to spend the larger part of the day shuffling papers in her office or so it appeared to me. She came out of her den to serve patients meals, and to dispense their medication if no experienced nurse was on duty. If she needed to speak to a member of staff, she poked her head round her office door and shouted, "Nurse!" If the wrong person appeared, she yelled, "Not you, the other". I do not think during the three months I spent on her ward, she once called me by my name. But calling for a nurse was the only time I heard her raise her voice.

We had been taught the practical aspects of dealing with a patient having an epileptic fit. Confronted for the first time with the reality of a person having a convulsion, was an unnerving experience. While attending to the patient, I sent a nursing assistant to inform sister. Nurse Lonner was a kind woman, who did not want to contradict me. She returned from the office reporting my senior's comment that all that was required from me were the names of the patients who had "fitted" during the shift. She needed this information, to fill in the ward report at the end of the day. I asked Nurse Lonner why she had not corrected me, when I had given her the wrong instruction. She replied that as a student I was her senior, she had not wanted to oppose me. I pointed out to her that she was the one with the expertise, and begged her not to let me do the wrong thing again. She seemed really cheered up by my comment, henceforth, we worked as a tandem and became the best of friends.

The sister ran the ward with the assistance of a long stay patient, who was in her confidence, and whom she trusted. As the only student on the ward, I was left in charge on Sister's day off. At the end of the morning duty, I handed the ward keys to the sister on the opposite shift. The trusted patient had given these to me in the morning. When we were on a late duty, a good half an hour before I was due to finish work, this woman started to follow me round the ward, endlessly repeating, "Hand over keys". I watched her one evening, and discovered that all the wards' keys, including the pharmacy's were locked in Mrs G's cupboard for the night. The only key the night nurse was trusted with was her own numbered passkey, which allowed access in and out of the ward.

Once a week we bathed all the patients. For the forty-eight people on the ward, Sister handed over a dozen pairs of underwear sets. She always reminded me to change only the dirty ones. This was allowing for the fact, that some of the patients had suffered convulsions during the week. They were afforded a bath and a full change of clothes, every time the episode had caused them to be incontinent. It seemed to me quite out of order, nevertheless, to dress patients in the underwear they had been wearing before their bath.

I risked mentioning my thoughts on the matter to Nurse Lonner expecting her to stand up for the system, but to my surprise she agreed with me. She confessed that since the war ended in 1945, a large stock of new underwear had been hidden by Sister. Apparently our senior had not understood that the stocktaking of patients' clothing had not been taking place for years. She was in fear of being found short of stock. When she went on holidays we dug up the hidden loot. We set about putting elastic in the knickers. They had indeed been part of the war stock when this precious material was in short supply. During these hostilities, in many institutions women's pants were kept up with the help of tape tied at the front. Some of the patients, who had not done anything constructive for years, were intrigued by our activities, and offered to help.

I was unable to explain to the sister on the opposite shift the reason for the diminished number of convulsions we had on the ward at that moment. Nurse Lonner said, "Maybe it is because some of the women have got something to occupy their minds, there is less quarrelling and irritation on the ward". In my ignorance, I thought that fits were only neurologically determined, and not a psychological manifestation.

But one thing, which may have had an effect on the patients nervous system was the effort I made to lower the noise level on the ward during my time in charge. The day space was an open plan, combining the sitting area and the dining room. The television set was switched on almost all the time. When I served meals, I had to shout to the patients above the noise to ask them their choice of food. I decided to switch off the set during the serving of meals. One of the younger patients objected. She complained to the consultant, Dr Redmond. He left me a note the next day telling me that the television was there for the benefit of the patients, not for my convenience. I had no right to deprive them of it. I wrote back a very polite note telling him that I refused to shout to patients at any time. I described my inability to serve meals, without having to do so with the set blaring. I invited him to come to the ward during lunchtime, and help me serve the food. Then, if he thought I should leave the television on, I would comply with his wishes. Not another word was heard from him on the matter. But he never came on the ward when I was on duty, for the remainder of Sister's holiday. I heard that the good Doctor referred to me as "the infamous Nurse Cobin", an improvement on OLD FLO, as far as I was concerned.

Dr. Redmond was a very handsome man in his fifties. He had worked at Worthfield since it opened in the 1930s. His only break from it had been the war period, when he served in the armed services. He had a sharp wit, which he exercised often at the expense of the other consultants. He was particularly hard on his colleagues who had started work at the hospital with him. As he was an Ulsterman he had done his duty during the conflict, while those who were from the South, enjoyed an accelerated promotion during the time he was under military orders.

He was especially acerbic when talking about the medical superintendent, whom he described as a two-ulcer-man with a one-ulcer-job. He could be brutally frank with the patients. To a long stay patient who asked him in my presence, "What is the matter with me Doctor?" he replied, "You are mad". So surprised was the woman that she laughed off the answer saying, "Oh! Dr. Redmond, you will have your little joke". The ward sisters idolised and feared him. I always knew him as, "God almighty Redmond". I could not say when or where I heard him being referred to this way, but I felt that the name suited him very well.

When sister returned from her holidays, we were rather worried about the unauthorised pillage of the linen stock. She accepted the "fait accompli" very sportingly. She was pleased that someone had dared to stand up to Dr. Redmond, and got away with it. I noticed that she started turning the television set off before serving lunch. But in reality I did not have much merit. It was always so much easier for me to be brave in writing, than to face a domineering person. When the time came for me to leave the ward, sister gave me her written report on my work. Apparently hidden in her office she had been aware of my efforts. Sister even came out of her den on my last day to share a cup of tea with us. She wolfed down a huge piece of Nurse Lonner's homemade cake, and was very friendly.

It was time for me to move on, but I was rather sad to leave the epileptic ward. I had become attached to some of the patients. I particularly liked the crafty ones, who had to be watched at medicine times. They were so quick at removing the wet pills out of their mouths, stuffing them all soggy into their pockets. I appreciated their quirky personalities. I admired the courage with which most of them endured their very disabling condition. During sister's holidays I had even become dependent on the faultless reliability of Mrs G's watchful eyes. More often than not, she would be the one who would warn me that Maggie or Theresa were stocking up their medication in the back of the linen cupboard or behind the lavatory cistern.

Chapter Twenty-Four

I was on duty on an admission ward, and thoroughly enjoying the stimulation of frequently having new cases coming in the unit. The one person I did not expect was Sarah, my erstwhile tormentor. She had returned recently from her second period of maternity leave. We were allocated to the same ward. But it was not a hostile Sarah who greeted me. She was smiley and friendly. I thought her change of attitude was due to her more junior status. She had been absent for two long periods on maternity leave. I was mistaken. The reason for her new amiability was because she needed a friend; one who could be trusted to keep a secret. When we had a quiet moment away from the flapping ears of our colleagues she confided in me. I was so glad that our enmity was over. It did not occur to me to rebuff her, however strange it seemed to have been chosen as the depository of her confidences. My relief at the cessation of hostilities was such that I would have done almost anything to maintain the status quo.

On Christmas day, many members of staff who were off duty visited their colleagues on the wards. The visitors expected to be offered alcoholic drinks, and a few mince pies. These nurses went round the hospital so long as they could remain upright, and hold a glass in their hands. Most of them were inevitably very drunk, long before the end of their visits. Sometimes old timers slept it off in a free side room, before resuming their boozy round. I never took part in these expeditions. If there was one thing I had learned from my years in Switzerland, it was work hard, play hard, but not at once or at the same place and not, if possible, with the same people.

The unwary on duty, succumbed to the temptation of having a few drinks with the visitors. This is what had happened to Sarah the previous Christmas. She got rather drunk. The ward sister was so busy entertaining the visitors that she was not very present on the ward. The patients had all, without exception, been given a little alcoholic drink with their lunch. Most of them were fast asleep in their armchairs. Sarah woke up from a snooze in a side room, but she could not quite remember getting there.

Shortly after Christmas, she was waylaid on coming off duty by a Portuguese student nurse. Salazar was a short, thin girl who would not have needed much theatrical transformation to play the part of Peter Pan. She told Sarah how much she had enjoyed the love session they had shared on Christmas Day. Sarah said she was a married woman, and such episodes could never have taken place. But the girl was adamant, and said she could not get the experience out of her mind. She wanted more. She reminded Sarah that she had been very drunk. Could it be that she could not remember what she had done, or how much she had enjoyed it? She even gave a detailed description of what Sarah had been wearing under her uniform. She accurately described anatomical details, a description of which, mercifully, I was spared. Salazar persuaded Sarah that she had been seduced, and she was very disturbed by it. She told Nurse Salazar that she had been too drunk to know what had happened. She did not want to repeat what she knew she would not enjoy. This was the wrong thing to say, as Salazar told her she would never know unless she tried once more. I had a strong feeling that Sarah had given in "just a little", thinking after that she would be left alone. But Salazar was still pursuing her. She appeared round corners, in the most unexpected places. She would never give up, and had said so.

What should she do? She said she was thoroughly confused, and no longer knew if she was Arthur or Martha. I sympathised with her, and assured her of my discretion. I could not offer her much help. She maintained that her marital situation meant that she was unable to seek professional help. I thought this might have helped her to clear her head. She had been heterosexually active since early adolescence. I felt that given the chance to talk this through, she would be clearer as to where she stood. After our shaky start at the start of training, and despite the difference in age, we became very good friends. I was frequently invited to her home, and was asked to be the godmother to one of her daughters.

My relationship with Paul Waver was rather like getting on and off a roundabout at the fair. I had been going out with him for quite some time when he told me his wife was back. I had not known that he was married. He told me that she had left him for such a long time that it did not seem important. However, as soon as he started divorce proceedings she returned. This had been the pattern for some years. My attitude was that while his wife was at home I refused to see him. As soon as she felt secure she left, taking all her personal belongings with her only to return the moment Paul restarted divorce proceedings. He had given me his word that he would tell me whenever she came back, but eventually he stopped doing so, and I stopped asking. I did not mention divorce or marriage. I never pressurised him in any way. Ms Casters was the one agitating about my peculiar situation. In her old fashioned way, she once said to me "I hope you are not making yourself cheap". The liaison went into years and did not fizzle out after a few weeks or months, as all the past ones had. She must have guessed that I was having an adult relationship with him. This was a distinct departure from the previous pattern of never allowing more than a few kisses, and occasionally some clumsy fumbling. The fear of pregnancy was always present in my mind. The Home Office was not tender with unmarried foreign girls who got into trouble. The next ferry or plane was their immediate destination. But after the traumatic break up with Eliot, I suffered from Amenorrhea, and my understanding GP had prescribed the contraceptive pill, which was allowed to unmarried women on medical grounds.

Ms Casters became irritated with Paul, saying once to me, "People do get divorces, you know!" As he was unaware that I knew the lady other than from work, he could not understand why she had become unpleasant towards him. He even complained to me about her change of attitude. I kept very quiet.

I would usually come to central London with him in the afternoon when I was off duty. I would leave him at his analyst's door, go shopping and meet him later for a coffee. When his analyst was on holiday, we sometimes went to his flat. We made love in the spare room. He could not understand why I would not lie in his marital bed. But I just could not. In any case I much preferred visiting him in the Mansion. He had a room there, which he used when he was on duty. I went in very discretely through the side door, and made my way upstairs. I could really have enjoyed myself there, if he had not always repeated, "Shush shush… Brother Montero", referring to the young doctor who was living in the flat next door. The young man was enjoying a torrid affair with a woman colleague many years his senior. I was quite sure, that these two had better things to do than to listen to us making love. But it was always, "Shush…quiet". A bit of a dampener.

At the end of the second year I was awarded two prizes. I had indeed causes to be pleased. My training was going well. I was not prepared for the hurricanes, which would shake my third year.

Shortly before Christmas, I was allocated to the mother and baby unit. This ward was the ultimate goal of all senior students. Three months in a ward, with young mothers and babies seemed wonderful. But it was not at all what I expected. For the first time since I had started my studies, I wondered if I was in the wrong place. The women were nursed in individual rooms. Some had their babies with them. But the extremely psychotic women, and the ones showing signs of rejecting their offspring, had their infants removed from them. These little ones were looked after in a nursery. They were kept away from danger until their mothers improved. The babies were reintroduced to their parent, very gradually, and under strict supervision. I could not get used to see mothers having to be watched, to make sure they did not injure their infants. One West Indian lady, who was said to be very positive towards her child, almost caught me unaware. I had left her singing a lullaby to the little boy. As I walked down the corridor, I noticed that the rhythm of the singing had changed. Without knowing quite why, I dashed back to the room. I dived just in time to catch the infant. His mother had been throwing him in the air. Another woman was making cooing and loving noises to her baby. She complained to the doctor because the child had been diagnosed as "failing to thrive. I looked through the peephole, and knew at last why the baby cried so much at feeding time. While trying to put the bottle in her baby's mouth, the woman would pinch him on the thigh. No wonder he cried. The baby was instantly removed. Within a few days he started to put on weight. This child was later put up for adoption. The mother, at last, felt able to own hating him. She even went home without taking leave of her child. I took it all too much to heart. I was very upset, but kept quiet. The ward sister, a middle aged French woman was unsupportive. She ignored me most of the time. She gave me her orders through the nursing assistant, a long timer on the ward. I worked, occasionally, with the Sister on the other shift, a very helpful and knowledgeable person. I tried to change shift occasionally with my opposite number, but after a few times, Nurse Garcia refused. She told me she would only work on my shift, if it were Sister Lenoir's day off.

I was in the ward's kitchen making myself a cup of tea when I saw a young woman I had not previously met. Thinking she may have come from another ward, I asked her who she was. She introduced herself as Fiona McCloud. She told me that she was a social work student. She was doing a three months placement at Worthfield. Was it all right if she made herself a cup of tea? While we sat down drinking our brew, I asked her if she knew the area. She gave me a negative answer. However, she owned up to be keen to get to know London, which was new to her. I felt a little bereft because Paul was away on study leave. I told her that I happened to have time on my hands for a couple of weeks, would she like me to show her the sights? She accepted my offer with alacrity. We arranged to go out the following Saturday afternoon. I told her the time of the Green line buses to central London. "Oh!", she said, "we won't need the bus, I have a car". I was a little surprised to see this quiet, gentle spoken person turning up in a mini van. I kept my reservations to myself, thinking perhaps that was what the poor woman could afford. My next cause for astonishment was when we went to a dress shop. She invited me to join her in a changing cubicle. She was just about wearing a flimsy bra and the tiniest of briefs. But the woman had been brought up in a British boarding school. I understood the attitude to nakedness was very different from the culture in which I grew up.

At the end of the day we went to a pub, and after a few drinks we confided to each other. She told me that her placement at Worthfield was a sort of probation. She had suffered a nervous breakdown towards the end of her course, and so she had failed to qualify. If she performed well, she would get her diploma at the end of term. If she did not satisfy her supervisors, she would have to rethink her future. I told her that I was on the last lap of my course, and that I thought that my love affair with Paul was on the wane. Luckily, I was quite guarded because I knew that she was working in the same department as Ms Casters, even if in a different division.

We saw each other frequently over the next few weeks. Usually after a few drinks, she talked very freely. Thus, I found out that this breakdown was not the first one, and that she had a long history of psychological problems. She thought she was about fourteen, when she went berserk in a hotel room during a holiday with her parents. She had well nigh destroyed the fittings. She had attempted suicide several times. She felt really well now, and was looking forward to her new life. I did wonder, however, how she had managed to get accepted on the course, after such a long history of serious troubles.

One evening, when we were sitting in my room listening to poetry, she suddenly put her hand out and grabbed my arm saying, "I am lonely, are you?" I removed my arm as I replied, "Everybody gets lonely sometimes". She said, "That is not what I mean". I told her that I was not interested in that sort of relationship. She said, "But we are friends, we get on well, don't we?" I agreed that we did get on well, but I could only go on seeing her if she kept her hands to herself. Upon which she promised that she would, if I stayed her friend. We had this conversation countless times over the next few weeks, as she became more and more frantic. Fiona's promises to behave appropriately were almost immediately followed by her making a grab for me. I felt very anxious and frightened that I might cause her to attempt to kill herself. She was obviously desperate to seduce me. She even changed her car, parking her gleaming new vehicle under my bedroom window. She slammed the door late at night so as to be sure to wake me up. Luckily, my two neighbours were friends. One of them,

Patricia Merton, was away in Ireland at the time, organising her forthcoming wedding. Martine Janot, my only French friend in Worthfield, was a heavy sleeper.

Paul was back, but I did not feel that I could talk to him about Fiona until the matter was resolved. My role in the relationship was to support him, not to burden him with my problems.

One weekend I was on duty, several patients had gone on leave. For once, the ward was very quiet. I had not answered my door, when Fiona banged on it the previous evening. So every time I heard someone coming into the unit I started to shake. When I got back to the nurse's home, Martine asked me to go to a concert. On our return, I stayed with her until it was time to go to bed. Then I retired to my room, and got ready for the night in the dark.

On Sunday morning, as I arrived on the ward I was violently sick. I felt ill all day. As the time wore on, I decided that I could not stand the situation any longer. I decided that I needed wiser council than mine, to help me clear my head. On coming off duty at five O'clock, I took the unprecedented step of telephoning Ms Casters. I told her I was very distressed. I could hear a lot of noise in the background. She said that she could not ask me to come over, because the house was full of people. There would be no chance to have a quiet conversation. She added that she had a free hour on Monday so we arranged to meet. I asked a girl who owed me a shift if she could oblige me, and work my duty on Tuesday. I arranged to go to the Pippins for two days, and I hid in Martine's room for the rest of the evening.

Ms Casters's reaction to my story was very firm and to the point. She said, "What she offers is not what you want, is it?" I said, "No, it is not". She then added firmly, "You are not responsible for this woman's life. If she decides to kill herself it is her decision. What she forgets is that she will not be here to see your face when you are told, and even if her death upsets you, in time you will get over it, but she will be dead". As I left her, she repeated, "Be firm".

When I returned to the hospital, I was in my room less than five minutes when Fiona appeared. She started to make a most horrendous scene, asking me to account for my absence. I stopped her very sharply, saying I owed her no explanations for my whereabouts. She said that I was making her feel like a leper. There was no point in being alive now. I steeled myself, to repeat word for word what Ms Casters had said, only adding, "Now get out of my room, I have to get ready for work. I do not want to see or speak to you ever again", upon which I opened the door, and she left. She did not return. I was moved at the end of the week to A division ward. There was little risk of seeing her suddenly appear there, when I was on duty.

I was still tormented by the fear of Fiona taking her own life. As the matter had been dealt with, I thought I might talk to Paul about it. One afternoon when we were walking through Portland Place, I was rather worried. He was going on about his wife, who was at last showing signs of independence. She had enrolled at London University for the next academic year. I had heard it all before so many times. Today, for a change, I wanted to talk about my problems. In this vast square, I suddenly felt alone. I had a severe attack of anxiety, and although I said nothing, he obviously sensed that something was expected from him. His reaction was to walk away, saying he had suddenly remembered an appointment. This man, whom I had been sustaining for years, left me in the middle of the street, the moment I needed his support. I knew then that I could never rely on him to be a steadfast companion through life. He had just demonstrated what I feared most in dependent relationships; suddenly finding yourself on quick sand when you thought you were on "terra firma".

Chapter Twenty-Five

I had to see my GP to renew my contraceptive pill prescription. I mentioned in passing that the bruising I had sustained on my breast when the senile lady had used it for support had become rather hard. I had not taken notice of it until it become painful. She examined me. I told her that the incident had taken place nearly three years ago. The breast had only been painful for a few months. The doctor was very concerned. She wrote a note to the specialist and giving it to me, she called a taxi. She pushed me into it, telling the driver to take me to the appointments' desk in the Out-patients Department of the Middlesex Hospital.

Several of the clerks remembered me, and a visit was arranged quickly. I saw Mr Hopkins a few days later. He could not say if the growth was malignant or not. This was both because of the way the lump presented itself, and the history of injury. I knew that I was to have an operation. The extent of the surgery would depend on the result of the frozen section, which would be tested in the operating theatre. A few days later, I was admitted to a ward I had so often visited when I worked at the hospital. News of my admission spread very quickly, I still knew so many people. I was treated with great kindness. If I had not been so anxious, I would really have enjoyed the spoiling after what I had recently been through. I had to sign a form agreeing to have a radical mastectomy, if the results of the frozen section warranted it. We were five women undergoing surgery that day. I was the only one who did not have a malignant tumour. When I woke up, and I knew I knew that I still had my breast, I kept repeating, "I am so lucky, so very lucky". The lump had been removed with such care that I was told the scarring would be well nigh invisible in time.

Dr. Redmond found out that my illness had deprived me of attending Patricia's wedding, and caused me the loss of my holidays in Ireland. He arranged for me to convalesce at his sisters' house in Dublin. I was touched by his concern while wondering what had demoted me from my infamous status in his eyes.

When the operation was over, Paul appeared with a bunch of flowers. He was about to be moved to work in the annex, a long way from the main hospital. I had already told him that I would be moving away to a flat in the next village, on my return from sick leave. He asked me to give him my new address. I said, of course, I would, but I had no intention of doing so. I knew it, and I think he knew it too. This was the last kiss and the final goodbye. We had never quarrelled, or even exchanged an unpleasant word. The relationship just died off, as the French put it so well, "en queue de poisson", in other words, tapered into nothingness.

My illness had prevented me from attending Patricia's wedding, but we remained friends. She worked in the experimental existentialist unit, as a therapist. Until her marriage, she had been accommodated in the nurse's home. I was only too happy to visit the young couple in the Mansion, where they had moved after their marriage. I had met her fiancé, Julian O'Flarty, a young psychiatrist who had recently transferred to the main hospital from the annex. Together with Martine, we had all enjoyed some jolly evenings. Martine had recently moved to the flat I was to take over. She said she wanted to be nearer to London, and she was prepared to commute. But as soon as I moved in the flat, it became obvious to me that she had no intention of going elsewhere. The rent was at the limit of what we could afford as nurses. The sharing of the flat on a permanent basis would have been tolerable, if the bedroom had been twin bedded. I was not prepared to share, even a king sized bed, except as a very temporary measure. I had it in mind to see for a few weeks how we got on living together. If all was well, we could ask the landlord for twin beds or to replace the rather worn sofa in the sitting room with a single divan, we could disguise with cushions. I kept my plans to myself for the time being. Martine had already been so cunning at getting me to share the flat under the pretence that she was about to go. Also, I knew her to be very impulsive. I was afraid that if I voiced my thoughts, she would jump the gun and speak to the landlord before we had a chance to see how things were working out. As it happened, I had been right to keep my own council.

Through my friendship with Patricia I had had the opportunity to meet on several occasions, some of the research staff from the experimental unit. We had some very stimulating discussions, on the way psychiatric patients were treated. This was with special references to the treatments inflicted on young people, suffering from what the staff of the unit insisted on calling "so-called schizophrenia". After one of these talks, the senior psychiatrist, Dr. Kierley, asked me what I intended to do when I had finished my course. I told him that I had started the training, with a view to enter the social work profession through the back door. However, having been so close to patients in my work as a nurse, I was no longer sure which way I wanted to go. It would be in psychiatry, as general nursing did not interest me. Dr. Kierly told me that I was far too intelligent to linger in the nursing profession. He pointed out that there were other areas of specialisation, if I wanted to stay close to patients. Dr. Kierly suggested that I could train as a psychotherapist.

It had never occurred to me that I could aspire to such heights. However, if this rather famous man thought I had the potential to do such a course, then this encouraged me. He told me, not to wait until I had finished my training to apply. By the time I would get the results of my nursing exams, I would have lost a year. I was recommended to the training committee by no less than Dr. Kierly. On the strength of it, and an interview, I was accepted. For the first two years the course demanded that I attend seminars one evening a week, and underwent a personal analysis, with an analyst approved by the organisation. I could attend most seminars, without too much difficulty. The week I was on morning shift it was simple, when I was on a late duty, it would be more complicated. But by changing my day off, and demanding the return of favours done to colleagues, I could manage most weeks. The analysis was a more serious problem. Most reputable analysts are far too busy to be able to offer flexibility of appointments on a regular basis. I tried several of them over a period of a few months, then I became discouraged, and put off trying a few more.

One evening at the seminar, I thought I recognised a young man I had seen around Worthfield. He introduced himself as Jake White, and told me that he too had thought that he knew me. It turned out, that he was doing research at the male experimental unit. He invited me for a meal after the seminar, and afterwards dropped me at the Green line stop. This became a weekly routine. Sometimes we went to Ronny Scott jazz club, which was most enjoyable. After my operation, and the break up with Paul, I felt that no man was ever going to look at me again. I found the friendship with Jake to be the balm, which I very much needed. I discovered quite by accident, that his father was one of the most famous men in the country. I was impressed by Jake's lack of pretension. He was driving a tatty red mini, and wore grandpa vests. He was always spotlessly clean, but his clothes were never ironed. He spent money most generously on meals and entertainments, but without any kind of ostentation. He lived in a large and sparsely furnished studio, very clean, like him. His home was in a part of West London, not too glamorous. I really appreciated the time I spent with Jake, and found the lack of pressure of any kind from him very healing.

One evening we were coming out of the seminar, when I found Martine Janot standing on the pavement waiting for me. It was hours after the shops had closed. I asked her, what she was doing there. She said she had been shopping, and coming out of the stores she had felt like a walk. She had suddenly found herself nearby, and decided to come and meet me. Jake said we were about to go to an Italian restaurant, would she like to join us. Throughout the meal she flirted so openly with Jake that at first I found it amusing, then embarrassing. I noticed that he was rather enjoying the game. When we rejoined his car, she pushed me into the back of the vehicle without much ceremony; and sat herself in the front passenger seat. Before long, it was obvious that she was having an affair with Jake. One evening as Jake and I came out of the seminar, she indicated very clearly, that I was not going with them by saying, "See you later" as she got into the car. She slammed the door, leaving me on the pavement. I could not believe that she could do this to me. She knew how vulnerable I felt at that time. Coming from a stranger this behaviour would have amused me; after all I was not in love with Jake, but from a friend it was very upsetting.

When I left for work the next morning, she was still sleeping. I spoke to Sarah after work. She said to me. "When I was unfaithful to Jimmy during our engagement he gave me a good thrashing. I know you can't do that to either of them, but do you have to go on living with her? Throw her out, or find yourself another flat". I had no intention of looking for another abode. As soon as I got home, I started packing Martine's belongings. I even took her pictures off the walls, and put the lot outside the flat. She was due to return at about 9.30. I thought, if she wants to sort this out, I am quite willing to talk. So I left the curtains open so she could see the lights. But by ten thirty, she had not returned, so I switched off all the lights and went to bed. When I left the house in the morning, I saw that her belongings were gone. She never spoke to me again. I was told by the Sister on her ward whom I knew well, that after work Martine had been invited to have a drink by a nurse on her shift, whose birthday it was. She took the last bus home, to find herself in the street at midnight. Everybody thought I had behaved very badly. Martine never forgave me, but Jake said to me, "You should not have taken the affair so seriously, she is only a Lolita. You are a woman, women are for keeps." But I thought, not this one.

A fellow student asked me if I had fallen out with Jake. I replied. "Not exactly, but he has been kidnapped by my friend Martine Janot." To which she retorted, "Oh! Well! another one for Ben, you know the pattern". No, I did not. "Jake has a fling, when he has had enough, he passes the girl on to Ben, so he is never encumbered. We were all amazed he took up with you, because you are so totally different from their usual little girls".

It was only then, that I remembered something Eva Kramer had said to me, referring to Martine years ago. It was during my ill fated drink party, that she had declared "The little girl is a devil, be careful!" I always wondered what had prompted the remark. I had thought that maybe she had played some teasing game on Eva.

I was working one afternoon a week in the Department of Out patients of the General Hospital in Worthfield's catchment area. Patients came for external consultations. Thus, avoiding having to make the long journey to the mental hospital. I was taken there by the senior consultant, and taken home by whichever doctor had finished his clinic last. When he was still at Worthfield, Paul was excluded from this obligation. This was both because he lived in central London, and added to his inability to control the length of his talks with the patients. He was always running very late. I very much enjoyed these afternoons away from the hospital. I usually got on well with the medical staff, who seemed to appreciate me. Dr. Redmond had a clinic, but he refused to let me do what he called "his donkey work". He brought the case notes of his list with him, and ushered his own patients into his consulting cubicle. He appeared promptly at 4 o'clock, when we all had a necessary tea break. If his wife, who was also a doctor, was on duty that evening, he sometimes invited me to the cinema. He introduced me to Bunuel, for whom he had a great admiration. On these occasions, he telephoned his wife in full hearing of all the other doctors. Speaking rather loudly, he asked her if her duty had been confirmed. Then he told her that he was taking me to the cinema. Paul never joined us for tea, as he was invariably trying to catch up with his paper work. However, he could hear the conversation. He usually looked furious.

Dr. Redmond always behaved impeccably towards me, and I thoroughly enjoyed these evenings. Once in June, he got out of the car, just as we were arriving at my home, picked a rose, gave it to me without a word and drove off. I was very touched, and kept a petal of the bloom in my Irish book of poetry. We had travelled a long way since the "infamous Nurse Cobin".

One afternoon one of Julian O'Flarty's patients did not keep his appointment. In the lull he had until the next person arrived, he asked me to come in. He shut the door of the cubicle. Without any sort of preamble, he told me that Patricia had left him. They had only been married five months. I took it that it was only one of these lover's tiffs, that newlyweds often have at the start of their married life. But he assured me, that it was more serious than that. She had told him that she hated him, marrying him had been a terrible mistake.

He then asked me to collect from the Mansion the papers I had left in their safe, when I went to have surgery. I had never retrieved them, despite frequent visits to the couple. I had also left a coat there, one evening after a rather well lubricated dinner. He meant to find a flat in London, and needed me to collect my belongings. I arrived at nine o'clock on the Saturday morning, as we had arranged. After a quick cup of coffee, I left. As I came out of the Mansion, I caught a glimpse of Chantale Kierly at her kitchen window. In a few hours, it was all over the hospital, that I had spent the night with Julian O'Leary. This was rapidly followed by assurances from people "who knew", that my affair with Julian was the cause of the marriage break up.

At the next out patient clinic, it was the turn of Julian to take me home. We had at that stage, not realised the extent of the scandal threatening us. When the clinic was over, he said he could not face returning to an empty flat, would I like to go out for the evening. We went to the cinema and enjoyed a meal out afterwards. He had discovered that the pictures on their walls belonged to me. He suggested that we picked them up on my way home. As we said goodbye, we hugged a little too closely. Things were in danger of getting out of control. I needed the comfort of some affection, but I did not think this was a good idea. I pulled away and Julian went home.

During the course of the following week, it became evident that the gossip far from calming down was taking on the proportion of a major scandal. Because of the reluctance of people to challenge a doctor, Julian still did not realise what was brewing. At the out patient clinic, he was again the one to end last and detailed to take me home. As it happened occasionally, none of the other doctors seemed to think it odd that the same psychiatrist would take me home on consecutive weeks. We went out again, and shared a bottle of wine. When he invited me to go back to the Mansion with him, I agreed. I thought that since everybody thinks we are having an affair, what is the difference whether we do or not. But it was not a very enjoyable experience, as I did not really like Julian in this way. I was well useless, and there had not been much in it for him either.

In the next few days the bomb exploded. I had been again allocated on Sister Loader's admission ward. But from being "la crème de la crème", I had become poisonous to the woman. Resisting her questioning, I had refused to gossip with her about my relationship with Paul. She could not very well say that I was bad at the job, after having poured praise on my head for so long. Instead, she set about destroying my character. I had been warned by a new consultant, Dr Berger, who shared his time between the main hospital and the annex. He had thoughts of recruiting me to work at the annex. It was in need of some renewed dynamism. He asked Sister Loader what she thought of me, and she had replied. "I could not talk more highly of her as a nurse, but I would not wish to discuss her character and personality, other than to say she is not a team player, and has no patience with her less gifted colleagues". That was the death knell to his idea, as in a small unit a lone rider would not fit in. By the time he had got to know me, he regretted his decision. But he had already offered the post to someone else.

By the time the next weekly ward meeting took place, Julian had already been tackled by his consultant about our supposed affair. He had denied that anything untoward had taken place. He reminded his superior, that we had been friends for some time. Sister Loader, having decided to embarrass me, asked us both in front of all the ward team, if we were having an affair. Julian denied it, and asked me to confirm it. I kept to what had been my firm line since I arrived at the hospital, and just refused to discuss it. One nurse, who was not usually friendly, asked if there was anything about my work that needed questioning. When told the standard of my work was not in question, she said that my private life was my affair, not the concern of the ward staff. She got up and left the room.

Inevitably, Mrs Cohen discussed the meeting in the social work's office. Ms Casters telephoned me, demanding I come to see her. Was there was any truth in the rumours circulating about Dr. O'Flarty and I? I was incensed by the interrogation, and I decided to lie to her. I told her about picking up my belongings, and that Mrs Kierley had started the gossips. She declared herself satisfied with my answer, but was nevertheless rather irritated, and expressed it. Worthfield was a very large hospital. Why oh! why did I always have personal dealings with people in her department? She then caught herself out, and said that she had meant to say her division. She worked in "A" division and Fiona McCloud in the "B" division. I guessed that her Freudian slip, had been her way of telling me that she had discovered the Lesbian who had pursued me, was a social worker. I had been very careful on discussing my problem with her, to avoid mentioning Fiona's name, or her profession. But somehow she knew who it was. I pretended not to notice her mistake. She announced herself satisfied with the meeting, which she declared to have cleared the air. I was thinking about the poem by Tennyson in which he says. "For a lie which is half lie is the foulest lie of all, for a lie which is all lie, can be met and fought with outright, but a lie which a half lie, is a harder matter to right". Even if having a single sexual encounter with someone did not constitute having an affair, the situation remained ambiguous. However, I was now over thirty years old, and my sexual behaviour should never have been a subject for public debate, and even less of intrusive inquiry.

I had successfully taken and passed both the internal and the state examinations. We never knew the grades awarded for the state finals. I had achieved top marks in the hospital tests, which was what was expected of me. All the other successful candidates were rushing off to do their general training, followed by the midwifery course. General nursing did not interest me. The thought of doing a Midwifery course, filled me with horror. In vain did the Matron encourage me, by pointing out that the SRN diploma was necessary for the progression of my career. She had to accept my decision.

Julian O'Flarty was very interested in the existential methods used in the experimental ward for young men. He decided to use a house away from the main hospital for his project. The property had been used as a half way house for chronic patients. These women did not need to be deprived of their independence. They cope well in external accommodation, with all their needs being financially met. The patients were able to do the work needed to keep the house clean, and put regular meals on the table.

With his usual determination, Julian ignored the advice of more experienced colleagues, as well as the injustice done to the residents of the house. He brought them all back to the hospital. He transferred to the lodging five disturbed adolescent girls. I was asked to take part in the experiment. Always willing to try something new, I agreed. I would be the only nurse residing with the girls. Guarantee of help from the other disciplines were given to the nursing authorities and to me. Occupational therapists, the patients' own social workers and medical staff in the person of Julian, were to relieve me regularly and give me support. However, it soon became evident that things were not going to go smoothly. Julian never made an appearance at the house. He contented himself with making the briefest of phone calls, and this at irregular intervals. I telephoned the head occupational therapist, who said that she was still waiting for Dr. O'Flarty to contact her. In any case, there would have been no question of her girls relieving me in the evening. As for the social workers, the only one who turned up, and stayed a few minutes was Fiona. I knew that Ms Casters had refused to get involved in what she called "a half-baked scheme". But where were the others? To avoid giving the impression to the girls that they were still in hospital, it had been decided that there should only be one nurse in the house. I was asked by Julian to wear civilian clothing. When no member of the other disciplines came to relieve me, it never occurred to me to discuss the situation with my nursing superiors.

I was on duty round the clock. I tried to maintain a reasonable bed time curfew. The girls were manageable in the daytime. But at night, I was kept up for hours by one or two of the them. I was not getting any rest, nor any break from the work. Over the week Julian's phone calls became shorter. Whenever I tried to ask to be relieved, I would be greeted with a remark such as "What is the matter with you? Can't you cope?" I tried to remind him that I was closeted in a five bedroom house, with very disturbed adolescents. This meant being on the alert twenty four hours a day. He said to me. "Nothing but your anxiety, is stopping you from taking time off and going out". I had by then been working the equivalent of three shifts daily for a whole week. So I arranged with a friend, to go out for a couple of hours in the evening. Before leaving the house, I informed the nursing administration that I was going out.

I was out for less than three hours. When I returned the house in an uproar. In my absence, one of the girls had taken an overdose of paracetamol. Thanks to the presence of mind of the most sensible girl in the group, she had been taken very quickly to the nearest hospital. I ordered a taxi, and took the remaining girls there with me. Jackie, the fifteen year old patient, had been given a stomach washout. She was conscious. We were all bundled in an ambulance, and sent home. The houseman and the ward sister were very sympathetic towards me; they gave me more support than I had received all week.

I stayed up all night to keep vigil. There was always a danger that this piece of acting out, would spark off some of the other girls into copy cat behaviour. But amazingly, it was the first night they all slept until morning. The next day, I was exhausted. Two days later, I had such a violent migraine, that I was unable to function.

I informed the hospital that I was ill, and would be leaving the house in two hours. No one came to relieve me, and I left. Anita Pipping took me home. When at last, I stopped vomiting and the pain in my head subsided, I slept for nearly two days. I telephoned Matron's office, and asked when I could see her. She asked me to come as soon as I felt able. I feared the worst. On meeting her I was shaking, and accepted the cigarette offered with gratitude. Her first remark was that she had asked me to come at once because she thought that I would be anxious to get the interview over.

Matron asked me to describe the last ten days. As I was talking she was obviously very displeased. I knew her anger was not directed towards me. She thought I had been ill treated, and decided that I deserved some compensation. It was not possible to reward me financially, but she thought a week's compassionate leave was more than due to me.

The whole episode could have been buried in the old Worthfield way. But that would have been counting without Dr. Redmond. He insisted on an internal inquiry to access what had gone wrong at the halfway house. I found the idea of appearing in front of people who would be looking for a scapegoat, rather intolerable. My Assistant Matron asked me if I intended to go. On the understanding that the absent are always wrong, I knew I had to attend the hearing. If I did not, I was sure to be blamed for the failure of the experiment. When

I arrived, I saw all the people who had been expected to support me were present. Julian started talking, attempting to justify his having dislodged the patients who were settled in the house. He seemed oblivious to the hard work it had taken for them leave the hospital. He then launched on a philosophical dissertation, about the need to avoid another generation of patients becoming institutionalised. As soon as Julian stopped to catch his breath Dr. Redmond said, "what we really need to know is what happened to Nurse Cobin in that house?" I had by then surveyed the room, and noticed that most people were avoiding my eyes. I knew I had them. The head O.T tried to justify herself, as did the social workers represented by Fiona. She made much of her impromptu visit. Every time one of them stopped talking, Dr. Redmond repeated his question. He eventually became rather irritated and demanded that I should be allowed to speak. I thanked him and went over the week, in the same way I had done with the Matron. I also corrected some of the gossip, which was going round the hospital. The most malicious was that I had left the house without warning the hospital, and disappeared. The Assistant Matron supported me, by adding that Matron was not worried. She knew how conscientious I was. She had been sure that I would contact her when I was ready, which I had done. On the way to the Nursing Office, the Assistant Matron praised me, for the professionalism with which I had handled the meeting. She said the Matron would not be disappointed. That was the last I heard of the episode. But Dr. Julian O'Flarty's resentment never abated, and would come out again, long after this incident was forgotten.

When I resumed duty I was allocated to a chronic ward as acting ward sister. It was a very comfortable posting; the patients were well trained. I had actually very little to do. The nursing assistant, who had been working on the ward for years, mostly acted as orchestra conductor. Beds were made, the ward cleaned, tables were laid and cleared after meals, without having to ask for the work to be done. She watched, observed and reported to me changes in the patients' behaviour. As I did not know them as well as she did, I may not have noticed subtle variations at first. She informed me that a certain Janet was always very tense before her periods. She was likely to explode if provoked. I was told that several patients were erratic during the full moon, which I pretended to believe. Occasionally, one of the patients "went up the pole". This was the Worthfield language for the occasional relapses, common in psychotic illness.

If handled with tact and understanding, these episodes were generally manageable. On her ward visit, the Matron was informed by a manic-depressive patient well on her way "up" that Sister Cobin was a really lovely person who should not be "crucified". People were after her because she had a boyfriend, naming a doctor from the male side whom I hardly knew. The Matron, to whom I had not spoken since my return to the hospital, reassured the patient that I could look after myself. I was rather embarrassed until I saw the smile on my superior's face, when away from the patient. This lady, a devout Irish catholic, never left the ward except on Sunday morning to go to church. I wondered where she got her warped information about me. But I understood why she would always ask me if I was all right. To my positive reply, usually came the swift retort, "they crucified Jesus, you know!"

After a few weeks of working in this very easy ward, I was bored. Having an easy time was fine for a short while. I was missing the adrenalin fix that more challenging units gave me. Apart from the daily visit by the Assistant Matron, the monthly visit from the Matron, we were not considered a unit worth bothering with. The ward doctor came once a week, unless a patient became disturbed and the prescription had to be changed. Even then, the chances were that he would ask me on the telephone to increase the phenothasine drug. Several of the women worked in other units as cleaners, or went to the Occupational Therapy Dept. They left the ward after breakfast returning for the midday meal. This was followed by a doze in front of the television until suppertime. After queuing for their medicines for the third time in the day, they either slumped in front of the television again or went to bed.

I had been in Worthfield long enough, to know how the system worked. Relief acting ward sisters were not expected to rock the boat. They had only to prove to everybody that they were flexible. They had to fit in the established ward routine, no matter how destructive

it was to the healthy part of the patient's personality. In that ward, as
in most wards on the women's side of the hospital, no one was unkind
to the patients. They were well fed, kept clean, encouraged to perform
domestic chores, spend hours daily watching moronic programmes on
television, given their medications, even handled kindly when they
had a disturbed episode. In other words, their lives were spent on the
perfect terrain for the flourishing of the institutionalised neurosis,
from which they all suffered.

But there was the occasional ray of sunshine in this peacefully drab
picture. The senior sister asked if I could find another job for Sally, a
young woman, who cleaned the patients' library. Instead of doing her
work, she found a book and took refuge in the corner of the room.
She squatted on the floor, her long hair covered her face, and read
time away. The librarian was displeased because the Department was
getting very dirty. When I went over to the library, I saw Sally's face
buried in a book of poems by Tennyson. I had never read this poet's
work. When I asked her what she liked about his poetry, I was amazed
by her intelligence and literary knowledge. This patient introduced
me to Tennyson, another joy in life. After the discussion I had with
the librarian, it was agreed that Sally would be allowed to take books
away from the department, once she had done her work. I was able
to present this package to the senior sister, who agreed to give it a try.
On the ward, Sally used to slump sideways in an armchair. Her hair
across her face and her nose in a book, she was oblivious of the rest
of the world.

A few months after I had left the ward, I was greeted at the bus
stop by a smartly-dressed young woman. She was carrying a large
suitcase. I had difficulty in recognising Sally as this elegant and
smiling girl. Questioning her on her destination, she told me she was
on her way to the airport. She was going to New Zealand to live with
her sister. Wondering if I was in the presence of a delusional
manifestation, I asked which airline she was flying on. Sally showed
me the ticket, which was still in the registered envelope her sister had
sent. I felt a little ashamed of having doubted her. Before getting on
the bus I thanked her for having introduced me to Tennyson, a gift
for life. I could not quite hear if she said, "he was the key", or "it was
the key". We waved goodbye to each other. I rang her former ward

the following day. I needed to know what had happened to Sally, to get her out of her semi catatonic state. The sister said, "Sally should never have been in this ward in the first place". But Dr. Redmond had said, "she will come out of it when she is ready, if ever".

Chapter Twenty-Six

I had decided to walk the three miles to my flat after work. I was feeling restless after yet another shift in which I had done very little. I had recently owned up to the director of the Psychotherapy Centre, that I had been unable to organise a personal analysis because of my difficult working schedule. I had not honoured the engagement I had made. This failure had resulted in my having attended the seminars for 18 months under false pretences. Dr. Graham's reaction had been too indulgent, telling me not to worry about it and that he would sort it out. This attitude made me feel that the organisation was not rigorous enough. I should at least have been given some sort of disciplinary warning. So I punished myself by leaving the course. I was now stuck in a professional "cul de sac". I suddenly realised that I could be running a chronic unit, or a tough psycho-geriatric ward for the next twenty-five years. Not everyone could be lucky enough to work in an admission ward, or one of the disturbed units. Patients, who had the misfortune of finding themselves in less glamorous areas of the hospital, had the right to be as looked after as all the other patients. I knew that somebody had to do it, but please God, not me.

The answer to my dilemma came to me in a flash. If I was to remain in the nursing profession, I must do the general training and qualify as an S.R.N. Much as the thought terrified me, I knew that without this qualification I would not get anywhere beyond the four walls of a long stay ward. I made an appointment with the Matron to inform her of my decision. Matron offered me a secondment on full pay, on the understanding that I would return to Worthfield at the end of the course. I accepted gratefully, as this made it possible for me to retain my independence, and live in my own home.

I settled on the Whittington Hospital, the biggest general hospital in North London, at the time. The hospital had been born from a "marriage á trois" at the creation of the National Health Service. The three wings had retained their individual character and culture. The unity of administration, uniforms and training school could not obliterate this. Even the food was different. The Highgate wing offered a superb breakfast to the night nurses, while main meals had a taste of home cooking in the Archway kitchen, and St. Mary's dining room offered the most generous helping.

The school of nursing had been modernised, and was very well equipped. The staff was dynamic and helpful. It offered me an oasis, where I could refresh myself after the ordeal of working in the medical wards. I could never get used to the numerous deaths of patients, which occurred in these units. Every time we lost someone, I dreaded having to deal with the body. But of course, I never said anything about my feelings on this matter. But one day, a ward sister refused to let the nurses do the necessary toilet to the body until visiting hours. This was over two hours after the patient had passed away. The statutory time was one hour, after which time the corpse rapidly became very cold, and I found it almost unbearable to touch. We had already lost two patients in the course of that morning. While other nurses could chat away about boyfriends, the last film they had seen, or just gossip, I just could not do it. I could never be casual about death. It was my weakness, and I never overcame it. This had decidedly been the cause of my reluctance to undertake general nursing. When it came to death, I was still the 10-year-old little girl who had been made to kiss the icy face of her beloved godfather.

The ward sister reported to the wing Assistant Matron that I had refused to obey an order. When I was interviewed by the lady, I pointed out that I had laid out two patients that morning and would have done a third one, if the proper procedure had been adhered to. This was ignoring the fact that asking me to deal with another dead patient was a little unfair. Two of the other nurses had done one each, the third, none. A few of the ward sisters were rather prejudiced against psychiatrically trained nurses. I had been warned that this sister was one of them. In most wards the prejudice against me vanished after a few days, but not here.

One of the two happy allocations of my general training was the time spent in the paediatric wards. Due to administrative errors, I was allocated there on three occasions. The mentality of the qualified staff was very different from the mindset of the general ward sisters. The nature of the work demanded a flexibility, which I could really identify with. It was fortunate that we never lost a baby or a child while I was on duty. The sisters in these wards thought I was "lucky". My first article, accepted for publication in the Nursing press, was the case study of a baby, so the unit had been lucky for me, too.

The other area in which I blossomed was casualty. I found there a renewal of the adrenalin stimulation, I had known in the acute psychiatric wards. The lack of a rigid routine, and the unpredictability of the days were very stimulating. We did lose patients. But the corpses were rapidly whisked away by porters. We had not known the patients before the emergency, and did not have to deal with the aftermath. The only really hard days were when we lost an injured child. But then, I found that comforting the distraught parents was the important task of the moment; it did not leave time for personal introspection.

I had been living on a ground floor studio flat in Highgate village. I decided to stay there, and commute to Worthfield when I finished my general training. Several of the West Indian nurses lived in North London. They managed the journey so this was possible. It was my first unfurnished home. When I rented it, the room had been in need of redecorating. So I set about painting it. For economy's sake I stuck to white, and borrowed a step ladder from friends. Anita Pippins turned up with a beautifully framed Raphael print from the Medici gallery. I had fallen in love with this picture the day I walked into her house, many years ago. She also handed me the receipt for a second hand gas cooker, which she had bought and which would be delivered to my flat. All the bedding was new, bought out of my savings. The remaining furniture was second hand, mostly Victorian, which I found in junk shops under the guidance of Anita. Lady Mary, a friend's godmother invited me to her house in Liphook. From there, we went on a fruitful expedition to Petersfield. A friend gave me a Victorian wing armchair, dusty, but comfortable, which she had found in the loft of her grandfather's house. I had repaired, stripped and polished all these pieces. The assembled puzzle formed the basis of a very comfortable home, in which I felt very much at ease.

What had been the back garden was full of builders' debris, which I set out to clear. I replaced the junk with a profusion of roses, daffodils and nameless shrubs. I bought these very cheaply in Woolworth in Archway. Most of the plants had lost their labels, and were the object of a special offer.

I returned to Worthfield and resumed the seemingly endless procession of relief duty. Most of the girls in my set, having gone to do their general training long before me, were now allocated to permanent wards as acting sisters. They all had their hopes set on the next promotion, which would see them full ward sisters.

By May 1968, I was replacing a French sister, who had gone home for her annual holiday. The posting, which was supposed to be for a few weeks, lasted beyond the time of the sister's official leave. The civil disturbances in France seemed to make it impossible for normal travel to take place. This locked ward was one of the two disturbed areas on the women's side of the hospital. It had the atmosphere of a beer garden rather than a therapeutic unit. For start, the noise level was unbearable. The television blared all day long, as if it were to be heard above the noise of the radio at the other end of the ward. No wonder the patients were irritable and easily aggressive. The sister on the other shift told me that it did not bother her. That is how this kind of ward was. I told the patients they could have one appliance on at any one time. Most of the residents accepted this restriction. If things went out of control, I quietly put the radio or the television out of order for a few hours by removing the fuse. Usually, I contented myself by turning the volume down without saying a word. Within a short time, the ward calmed down. Even the assistant matron commented on it during her round. Some patients started coming to the sister's office. They began talking to me about their problems and worries.

One such a patient was Becky. She was an extremely beautiful young woman of thirty-two. She reminded one of Kim Novak. Becky had been suffering from depression. She had spent sometime in the admission ward, and had been transferred to the disturbed ward, because she was not recovering. Her medical notes said that this patient seemed unable to disclose any worries or severe emotional upset. It had to be assumed that her depression was endogenous. She was not psychotic, not at all the sort of patient usually found in a disturbed ward. I gained her confidence. She told me that she was feeling very guilty because she had worked as a part time prostitute for some years. Looking at her notes I discovered that she had a very good job in one of the top London fashion houses. So I asked her why she needed the extra money. She said she was saving to buy a home, as she could no longer stand the insecurity of living in rented accommodation. Every time a landlord came for the rent, she was convinced she would be asked to go. She then explained that she had been abandoned as a small baby. She had been fostered by a couple, who had been very loving towards her. By the time she was about four or five, the apparently sterile woman had given birth to twins. Becky was returned to the care of the Social Services. She never saw these people again. She had spent the rest of her childhood going from one foster home to another. When she was about twelve, she had asked a social worker why her early foster parents had "got rid of her". The answer had been that now they had two babies of their own they did not need her anymore. During her adolescence, she was placed in a family who took good care of her. They ensured that she had the best education possible. This enabled her to get the job in the fashion house. She was gradually promoted as she became more experienced. But her salary would never be enough to enable her to save for the deposit most building societies expected from prospective house buyers. She said that all the years she had spent with the last family, she had never ceased to fear being discarded again. She had been sure that if she had a home of her own she would at last feel safe. So she became a part-time prostitute and saved up her earnings. But as soon as she had enough money to put a deposit on the home of her choice, depression overtook her. She could never forget how she had earned the necessary capital.

I was on late shift and the London train was delayed. When I got to my destination, I found that I had missed the bus, which would have taken me to the hospital. So I walked the couple of miles up the hill to get there. I arrived ten minutes late. The sister on the other shift had already gone off duty. She had given the ward keys, including the keys of the ward pharmacy to the experienced nursing assistant who had passed them on to the 18-year-old student. I found the young nurse sitting at my desk reading the morning's ward report. She handed me the keys and having greeted the patients, I returned to my office to inform myself of the morning's happenings. Within a few minutes a patient walked in and said, "Becky is on the floor of the dormitory saying she does not feel well". To which I replied, "If Becky wants to speak to me she knows where I am". But I got up and went to see her. She was indeed sitting on the floor, and looked very unhappy. When I asked her what had happened, she told me she had taken an overdose of Largactil tablets. I said, "but how could you if you are not on Largactil?" She said the student nurse had given her the bunch of keys. It turned out that she had asked the nurse for a packet of sanitary towels and a pint of milk to make tea. The student had given her the keys, and told her to help herself. In that ward all the keys were tied together in a single bunch. This was not only strictly against hospital rules, but also against the law. So to open the cupboard where the stores were kept, all the keys had to be handled. I never gave the keys to the patients. However, it was not my place as a replacement sister to alter the system operating in the ward.

I called the ward Doctor who said he would be here soon. He sounded as if he had been taken out of a deep sleep, or was it an alcoholic doze?. I waited for a little while as I was hunting round the ward for normal saline. We would need this to give Becky a stomach wash out. There was none on the ward, neither was there the necessary equipment to perform such a procedure. In desperation, I mixed salt with water and forced Becky to drink it. She vomited a little, but by then it was obvious that the drugs had already began to be absorbed into her system. It took the ward doctor forty five minutes to appear on the ward. He decided to call an ambulance. Becky was taken to the Casualty Department of the nearest general hospital. There, she was the victim of additional medical mishaps. She died in the middle of the night.

News of Becky's death spread like an Australian bush fire. I had barely set foot on the ward the following afternoon, when I was confronted by the Coroner's officer. It was quite terrifying, to be interviewed like a criminal by this man in police uniform. I had to describe second by second, all my moves and every word I had uttered from the moment I had set foot in the ward the previous afternoon.

But it was just the start of the harassment. The next afternoon an irate union official called on me. He was furious because I had not called him. He explained that lawyers may need to be summoned to stand up for the staff. The student nurse, who did not belong to the union was made to join, so she could benefit from the service of the solicitor. In the end we needed the help of a barrister. We discovered that the hospital management committee had taken a QC against the ward staff. The administration was anxious to prove that the policy of the hospital for the care of the keys was not faulty. In their opinion, the correct procedure had not been implemented by the nurses.

Matron was away on holiday, and the deputy was not much help. I told her that the union had said that I should have accused the patient of having broken down the door of the pharmacy. But it had never occurred to me to lie. The lady said without conviction. "Of course, you should not lie". It was obvious that she agreed with the union man. I had to repeat my statement so many times that the slightest inaccuracy would have been noticed. I was going home with the words, keys, a bottle of milk, sanitary towel buzzing in my head. My only source of comfort was the fact that I had done all the right things in the light of what I knew. But my worry about the unorthodox saline procedure reached almost unbearable pitch, when I heard the Coroner describe the causes of Becky's death. I had been right in thinking that Largactil had already been absorbed when she reached the general hospital. Her stomach showed some bleeding, which was consistent with the first aid treatment she had been given. She had cardiac arrest in the general hospital. Then a junior doctor injected her lung instead of her heart, consequently causing her death. The inquest was adjourned for six weeks. On hearing this I nearly fell over.

When the verdict came, the cause of Becky's demise was declared to be death by misadventure. The case having being commented on in the press, suddenly long lost relatives appeared. They started a battle royal with the only people who had apparently cared for Becky, the last family where she had been fostered. They fought over her money, her jewellery, even her clothes. I expressed some anxiety over the possibility that the hospital might be sued by these people over the general treatment meted to Becky. The union man was right, when he said that they were too busy fighting over her belongings. No one would bother to ask questions as to what had happened to her. No one ever did.

I was grief stricken, as were several of the women on the ward. Without staff realising it, Becky had made herself indispensable to some of the chronic patients. She made endless cups of tea, generously shared her cigarettes and her chocolates. She ran errands for the inmates who were not allowed out of the ward on their own. My sadness eventually abated, but I never totally got rid of the guilt. I became convinced that if my train had not been late, I would have been on the ward a good twenty minutes earlier. This tragedy would have been averted. I also felt guilty about the level of anger I had felt towards Becky, as I forced her to drink the saline, hoping it would make her vomit sufficiently to save her life.

Nearly twenty-five years after Becky's death, I accompanied a friend to a spiritualist service. The meeting was going to be attended by mediums. My purpose had been to prove to Celia that the set-up was fraudulent. The decision to go had been sudden. No one knew we were coming. After the passing on of "messages from dead relatives to members of the congregation", the medium came down from the podium. Walking towards me, she said she was having a strong need to speak to someone she thought was called Claire, or very near that. The message was from Rebecca who had lived in Kilburn, and had passed away some years ago. Rebecca said that Claire had looked after her when she was ill. The message was that she was very sorry, that she had not really listened, and used the help offered. She knew Claire was still helping a lot of other young people. But now, the time had come, when she needed to look after herself. I knew it was Becky. She did live in Kilburn, and Rebecca was the name by which she had been officially known. Claire was so near to Clara that I had to accept that the message was for me. Becky had been very far from my mind at that moment, as I had recently been bereaved. I had vaguely hoped that if there were anything of value in the séance, my recent loss would manifest itself. I was also trying to make decisions about retirement, after many years in the caring professions.

When the Matron came back from her annual leave, she asked to see me. It was with some understandable trepidation, that I directed myself towards her office.

She asked for my verbal account of what had happened to Becky. When I had finished, she said that when all was said and done, taking the Largactil had been the young woman's decision. We are all in charge of our own lives, and killing herself had perhaps been the result of Becky's guilt about the prostitution. She wanted to know, why no mention was made of this activity in the patient's records I was impressed, to hear that she had perused nearly a year of psychiatric notes since her return. I explained that Becky had not been able to talk to the psychiatrists about this aspect of her life. Matron very astutely thought maybe this was because they were all men. I refrained from telling her that she had not spoken to the nurses either, as this would have been a reflection on my colleagues.

They had failed to gain her trust. She had trusted me, but much good had it done her.

Before I left her office, Matron told me that from the first of May, I had been promoted to the rank of full ward sister. It was only because she had been away that I had not been informed before. She wanted me to go to the linen room at once, to be kitted with the appropriate uniform. The sewing mistress was waiting for me. The next day a group of very important visitors was to come to the hospital. She wanted me to escort them for the day. "It is important to me", she said, "to know that everyone is aware that I have total trust in you". Her last words to me were that the assistant matron had given her details of my articulate handling of the QC. But all I had done was answer on my own behalf, "No, I do not allow patients to handle the ward keys. As for the other shift, I had never worked with them. The staff will be in a better position to answer this question, Sir".

News of my promotion came as great a shock to the group I had trained with. The girls had mistakenly thought that because they went to do their general training while I stayed in Worthfield, they would be promoted before me. They forgot that during the time they were away, I had given service to the hospital, and acquired experience. The result of my elevation was that my isolation increased. I was the victim of ridiculous pettiness on the part of my colleagues. Most of them lived in North London. When we were on duty in the morning, we were all collected in a sort of cattle truck from the railway station. We had to make our own way back to the station, at the end of the shift. In the afternoon there was no hospital transport to collect us from the station. We made our own way on local buses. The West Indian set, formed a very cohesive group.

They usually came to work by public transport. Husbands and living in lovers collected them in the evenings. Until I was promoted, I was often picked up at the bus stop, and given a lift to North London. I would be dropped either a few minutes walk from my flat, or a short bus ride away. This would get me home shortly after half past nine. If I travelled wholly by public transport, I arrived home around ten thirty. After my promotion, the girls used to get their men to slow the cars as they passed the bus stop, wave at me, then speed on. As if to prove her trust in me, after a short time spent on relief, I was at last given my permanent posting. This was the second disturbed ward on the women's side of the hospital. It had the advantage of being an A division ward which I preferred.

Ms Casters had retired while I was doing my general training, and a new social worker was working with Mrs Cohen. Fiona McCloud was now on the staff. It would have been impossible to avoid her, if I had been working in "B" division. She had behaved correctly, on the rare occasions I had had professional dealings with her. I was still afraid that continually having to meet her, would have been more than either of us could handle.

Disturbed Ward A treated the same type of patients that I had met in Disturbed Ward B. I had been allocated there as a student. It was a distinct advantage, as I already knew most of the long stay inmates. There was also in the unit a fair number of acutely ill new patients. The ward was a lively place, but it was not a beer garden. I knew the other sister from having worked opposite her for some months in another ward. Sister O'Leary was a quiet Irish woman, whose personality promoted an atmosphere of security in the unit. She never left the ward before I arrived. I always waited for her if she was a little late. We had a very smooth working relationship.

Many of the patients were extremely obese. This was a side effect, of the large doses of phenothiazine tranquilisers they were given. This added to the lack of exercise and caused some of these women to weigh over 20 stones. The ward doctor asked if we were willing for a group of women to take part in a slimming drug trial. Sister O'Leary and myself agreed to encourage the patients to participate in the experiment. The women were also put on a weight reducing diet. The rewards offered to them were to be 10 cigarettes if they were found to have lost weight at the end of any week. The most enticing prospect for some of them was the promise to be taken shopping in the nearby town. They would be allowed to choose a new outfit, every time they had reduced their poundage by two sizes. Most of the women had not been in a shop for many years. They were keen to have a go. But Sheila a five foot one inch woman of 18 stones was mostly looking forward to the improvement of her sex life. She told me that men could only take her from behind, because she was so fat. She added that her weight also made it difficult for her to "mashpatate".

When the time came to go shopping, we took three patients to town by taxi. As we got out of the car, one of the women pulled up her knickers in the middle of the street. The rest of trip went well, until we took our charges to a hamburger bar as we had promised. We had told them they would be allowed to eat what they fancied, as a one off. One of them Mary, told the waiter she wanted a fried egg with salad, saying firmly, "No chips". When her food came, her dish had the forbidden item on it. Mary took the plate with both hands and shook it in the air, shouting, "I said NO FUCKING CHIPS". The waiter looked at me, appealing for my support. But I said firmly, "The lady had said no chips". He removed the offending plate. When he returned the food to Mary, she greeted him with one of her rare smiles.

The great range of diagnostics we had on the ward demanded vigilance at all times. Whether it was keeping an eye on the Tuinal addict, or the "carver" always waiting for a second's distraction to cut herself. We were on the alert at all times. The ward doctor, a Middle Eastern gentleman, was a pill pusher. Mercifully, he was not an apostle of the ECT box. He spent very little time on the ward so my relationship with Sister O'Leary was very important. I found it impossible to relate to this man, who thought that all psychological problems were due to chemical imbalance in the brain. His only interest in the ward was to sign the medicine cards. Sister O'Leary was more philosophical. "These young doctors, they come and go, I give him six months". She was right, six months it was. Shortly before Christmas he left, but I did not rejoice when I heard that the replacement was going to be Dr. Julian O'Flarty. Remembering the past we shared, I feared the worst. He had by then divorced Patricia on the ground of desertion. Julian had remarried, an artist whose talents did not stretch to sewing buttons. He used to come to the ward in the morning, handing me a cardigan or a jacket with a button loose or separated from the garment. I would not sew for him, thinking that I was neither his mother nor his nanny. He always found a nurse, willing to find a needle and thread. Sometimes when he came in, he asked for breakfast. If we were having our break, I would look at the nurses. One of them usually volunteered to organise him some nourishment.

Chapter Twenty-Seven

In November I was away for three weeks on a management course. The morning I returned I was cornered in my office by Paula. This young woman, suffered from paranoid schizophrenia. She had been transferred to Worthfield from another institution. As a result of her extreme violence, the previous hospital had wanted to send the girl to Broadmoor. Her parents had begged the consultant at Worthfield to give her another chance. We had so far managed her well. But that morning without any apparent provocation on my part, she started to hit me about the head. She scratched my face, with nails that the nurses had forgotten to keep short while I was away. I was trying to escape, when she grabbed my collar and bashed my head against the wall. I called for help, but the two tiny Asian nurses who were on the ward with me were no match for Paula. They ran away when I succeeded in freeing myself, I found that I had two deep scratches running from my forehead to my chin. I could not feel the back of my head. The scratches on my faces were very painful. I rang the Nursing Office, to speak to the unit assistant matron. All she said was, "But you sound all right, now".

I worked until Sister O'Leary came on duty at two o'clock. After she had seen the back of my head, she advised me to see my GP without delay or go to casualty. My doctor was appalled that I had been left to cope with such an incident without any help. She said the back of my head was like strawberry jam. She cleaned and disinfected my injuries, and forbade me to go to work for a week. When I resumed duty, the assistant matron excused herself. She said that when she had done her round the day of the assault, she had not seen the back of my head She had only noticed my grazed face. I answered that I had not either, my eyes not allowing me to see that far. She retorted, that there was no need for me to be sarcastic.

Paula greeted me with a perfect schizophrenic remark saying. "I forgive you for hitting you, even if it was your fault. You know, that wives should not go away without telling their husbands. As my wife, it was your duty to warn me that you were going away". It was true that I had told the patients as a group that I would be away for a while. However, not being aware that I had become part of Paula's delusional system, I had not made a special point of informing her.

When they visited Paula, her parents were more concerned about the possibility of Paula being transferred to Broadmoor, than about my injuries. To placate me they showered me with expensive presents. All of them, whether it was the handbag or the jewellery, were of a size, which would have looked big on a ten tons Tessie. These gifts looked distinctly comical, on a woman who had a struggle keeping on the positive side of eight stones.

Shortly after this incident I was attacked by the "carver". I had tried to stop her from butting the window with her head. To my amazement I threw this 5 foot 9 inch woman over my shoulder, and fell on top of her. I did not injure myself in the fall. The damage had already been done. Jean had kicked my already fragile knee, with a foot encased in plaster of Paris. Her four limbs were protected in this way to stop her from picking at her stitches.

One very positive aspect of the culture, which had been prevalent in Worthfield was gone. The old Irish contingents and the young West Indians nurses had always helped in violent emergencies. But, there had been a sudden influx of tiny Asian nurses. Some of them were very understandably frightened of the violent patients. It was unfair to put them in this situation, because so few of them had the strength to help. In a crisis, they endangered themselves and all of us. As I limped my way around the ward, I began to wonder if the game was worth the candle.

I had agreed to be on duty from Christmas Eve until Boxing Day. It was important for Sister O'Leary, to be with her children at this time. On coming off duty, I went straight to the Pippins. Anita had staged a "little Christmas" just for me. On my return to the hospital, I was shocked to find sitting in the sister's office, no other than Sarah's pursuer. I had met Staff Nurse Salazar, when I was acting ward sister. I had coped well, with her ambiguous remarks about my legs. She wrongly declared them to be the most beautiful ones in Worthfield. She was only a student then. I could relatively easily deal with her. Usually, I gave her an order, which got her out of the office. In any other hospital, I could have handled it in a much more disciplined manner, but it was not Worthfield's way. The deputy matron lived well up to her nickname of the "students' social worker". Her protegees could do no wrong. I could not complain to the matron about such petty nonsense.

But now the girl was acting as ward sister, dealing with her could prove more difficult. I decided to ignore her barely coveted sexual remarks. Surely, she would eventually get the message. Sister O'Leary had slipped on the ice on Boxing Day. She had sustained a complicated fracture of both tibia and fibula. My colleague was expected to be away for up to four months. I hoped the girl would not keep this banter up that long. She had never let go of Sarah. The question really was, did Sarah really want to be left alone? I was no longer so sure, but I kept my doubts to myself.

It was not long before Salazar restarted her onslaught of remarks about my lovely legs. In fact I did not have lovely legs. I never had nice legs. They were heavy and short, and not really in keeping with the rest of my slender physique. This made her continual references to them, all the more irritating. But much more serious concerns were occupying me.

We had on the ward a very tragic patient. Mrs Salmon's condition was in large part, the result of two failed leucotomies. This poor woman had been tormented by a severe obsessive neurosis. Her disorder resisted all therapeutic attempts. So the decision had been taken to operate on her brain. Having failed at the first intervention, she was operated on again. This resulted in severe damage to her personality. She had been an over anxious but gentle person. She was now a very irritable, demanding and sometimes verbally aggressive woman. She was transferred from the private clinic where she had been treated to a National Health Service hospital. She never attacked anyone, but her rasping, insisting voice could be heard all over the ward, if she was thwarted. She was a middle class Jewish woman, who may have been rather indulged. Her brother-in-law was a prominent politician. This man had largely taken over keeping an eye on Mrs Salmon. Her broken hearted husband had felt unable to cope with the poor woman alone. His personal assistant visited the patient monthly, bringing her cigarettes, toiletries and clothes as needed. It was a beautiful dressing gown this woman had brought Mrs Salmon, which acted as a catalyst. It brought home to me that all was not well in the way the patient was treated on the other shift.

I had already noticed that since Sister O'Leary's accident, Mrs Salmon was often mentioned as disturbed on the report. One day, I came on duty for the afternoon shift, and found the ward unusually disturbed. It seems that Mrs Salmon had set fire to her room. Salazar said that the patient had been impossible to manage during that morning. The staff had decided to send her to her room, and locked her in for the rest of the shift. Unfortunately, they had not taken away her matches. She had used then to set alight magazines she had stored in her locker. It was her banging on the window, which alerted passers-by. They saw the flames, and raised the alarm. The room was not damaged but Mrs Salmon had sustained some burns to her hands. She had been holding the lighted magazines to the window. The punishment, which had been inflicted by Salazar, was that the patient should lose her room and sleep in the dormitory. But it really was not a decision that could be made by relief staff. I insisted in investigating the facts, which had led to the crisis.

I interviewed Mrs Salmon. She told me that she was being bullied by the staff on the other shift. She said that if she asked for a packet of her own cigarettes, the answer was always, "Later we are busy," even if the staff were all sitting over a cup of tea.

I knew well this trick of Mrs Salmon, to ask for something as soon as she saw the nurses attending to another patient, or having their break. I tried to get round it by telling her that I would be seeing to her in so many minutes. So long as the waiting time was not set too high she waited, with her eyes on the ward clock. The tip had been given to me by Sister O'Leary. I had passed it on to Salazar who had chosen to ignore it. Mrs Salmon told me that she had been dragged on the floor, all the way from the sitting room to her room. As all the ward floors were polished, I asked the lady to get up, and turn round. I saw that indeed the back of her beautiful dressing gown was coated with floor polish. Looking closer, it was obvious that this piece of bullying was a recurrent way of dealing with the patient.

I would have been appalled if this treatment had been dealt to any patient. The thought that Mrs Salmon would tell her visitor about this ill treatment caused me to be very worried. There was no point in demanding the help of the new Assistant Matron on our shift. She belonged to the Hispanic mafia. She was always dismissive of me, and of any suggestions I made.

I thought we should have a general ward meeting, and informed Julian O'Flarty of my intention. He said he would attend. The nurses on my shift agreed to it, while grumbling that the incident had nothing to do with them. They did not ill treat anyone. After I had explained the purpose of the meeting, I launched on a resume of the number of times Mrs Salmon had been reported as being exceptionally difficult over the last few weeks. One of my nurses piped up, But not often on our shift". To which Salazar retorted, "What are you implying?" This was said in such an aggressive tone that my nurse backed down by saying, "Maybe she just misses Sister O'Leary, she was used to her". After this put-down, every time one of my nurses started the apology of our shift, she was quickly either seduced into a retraction of her remark, or simply intimidated out of it. Julian and Salazar were exchanging broad smiles. No amount of effort on my part could bring the meeting to a constructive discussion on the matter at hand. Deciding what would be the best way of helping Mrs Salmon, while avoiding the pitfall of treating her like a VIP. I had kept what I thought was my ace for the end. I asked if it were true that Mrs Salmon's burns on her hands had not been treated for over thirty minutes, after she was freed from her room. All the staff on Salazar's shift started to shout at once. The only two words I could distinguish were "not urgent". Unfortunately, by then I was so irate that I sniggered, "Not urgent! Ah! Ah!", which annoyed Julian O'Flarty. Even my nurses looked ill at ease.

After the meeting Julian came into the office. He shut the door, and began to berate me in a way that showed his resentment towards me had not abated. Fishing from the existentialist vocabulary he had gleaned along the way, he told me that what I was doing to the nurses was appalling. I was double-binding them in a disgraceful manner. Mrs Salmon's needs were never mentioned. When he opened the door, we found that my nurses had been standing in the corridor, listening to every word he had thrown at me. Hearing the ward doctor berating me, my staff lined up with Salazar, and would not speak to me again. Almost all the ward nurses sent me to Coventry. One Spanish nurse, remained friendly and loyal to me.

I did ask her why the other nurses on my shift were behaving so badly. Without hesitation, she replied, "They say you do not care about the staff, you only care about the patients, and you always say that is what we are here for". I saw the extent of the hostility toward me, when I asked a student nurse to special the "carver". I saw her walking in the opposite direction from the patient. I called her to order, but when she said to me "You better fucking well do it yourself". I knew I was beaten. I did try to enlist the help of the Deputy Matron, by asking her to remove the student from ward A. Her reply to me had been "Poor girl, she cannot be well to speak like that, be patient". I replied "Well, Ms Leroy, if I have an extra patient on the ward, and one less nurse can you give me another student, to make up the staff number". The lady retorted. "What is the matter with you Sister, can't you cope?"

We admitted a very disturbed woman. She smashed several dining chairs, after which she collapsed in my arms in tears. As it was an emergency, I went to see the Matron directly, needing her agreement to order some replacement furniture. I mentioned to her in passing, that I had seen in the nursing press that St. Dymphna's Hospital on the other side of London was advertising for two assistant matrons. I had not consciously thought of applying. I had not been a sister long enough to aspire to such a promotion. In any case the position of Sister Tutor was more likely to be of interest to me when I was ready. But when the Matron said, "I would be very sad indeed to lose you. As you well know we need capable people here, but you can go to the very top of the profession if you choose to, only your inner insecurity can stop you from getting there". I felt stung by the remark. I thought. "I will show you, if I am insecure". I decided to apply for the post. Less than a month later, I was giving Worthfield my notice to quit. I had not even repaid the years of service I owed the hospital. But no one mentioned it.

Chapter Twenty-Eight

St. Dymphna's hospital afforded me a severe cultural shock, when I took up my post. I could not expect the same mentality from the staff of an institution, which had been in existence since 1830, to be a carbon copy of Worthfield. The buildings were mostly Victorians. A few bungalow wards had been added in the 1950s. Wooden structures, which had been built to house the casualties in the First World War, completed the accommodation for the patients.

The first thing one became aware of on starting work in St. Dymphna was the disciplined way in which the hospital was run. One did not see patients wandering round the grounds in a dishevelled state. If inmates were seen walking outside on their own, it was because they had been given ground parole. They were correctly dressed, and their walk had a purpose. If they attempted to pass the gates, and go to the village, they had to produce a small passport. This stated that this person had been declared fit by the medical officer to leave the hospital on his own.

Unlike Worthfield's personnel, the staff at St. Dymphna did not spend a lot of time attending the Coroner's Court. Suicides were rare, and when they did occur, there was no attempt at brushing the tragedy under the carpet. It was used as an excuse to tighten the system a little more. Questions were asked, and consciences examined. It was always taken very seriously. Even when the tragedy had nothing to do with your area of responsibility, you were made to feel guilty.

The female nursing staff was managed very strictly. Uniform dresses had be a certain length and of course, spotless. Belts should not be held by safety pins, and fancy shoes, even of the right colour were not tolerated. Time keeping was, of course, of utmost importance. Nurses, who were late on duty had to report to the Deputy Matron. In the morning, sharp at 7 am, the Assistant Matrons called their wards to check that all the staff had come on duty. When I suggested that it maybe simpler to ask the ward sisters to let us know if someone was missing, my idea was received with scorn. So I went on making ten mostly useless telephone calls every day.

The Matron Ms Mildred Pincher, was of a cut tailored on the Florence Nightingale pattern. Her regime was totalitarian. No discussion was ever tolerated, let alone contemplated. Every attempt one made at what seemed to be a constructive suggestion was met with one of two responses. Either, "It can not be done", or, what was even more infuriating, "If it was necessary, we would have done it a long time ago". Insistence would only cause the lady to launch on a short speech, explaining why things were as they were. They had to stay as they had been since the hospital opened as the Morwell Asylum in 1834, and as such they had served the community well. This oratory invariably ended with Ms Pincher hitting her desk with a clenched fist, while declaring, "It is as simple as that!" So ended any attempt at bringing the hospital into the 20th century. The Matron's authoritarian attitude gave my manipulative inclinations plenty of scope to be truly imaginative. Useless to attempt what was needed for modernising the mentality of the 19th century institution. However, against the most rigid resistance, I did manage by devious routes to obtain certain minor physical changes.

To achieve what I saw as improvements, I made friends with the skilled men who kept the structure of the hospital in good repair. So while my colleagues where paying court to the higher echelons of the hospital hierarchy, I had cups of tea with the carpenters, the electricians, even the upholsterer. I could do little to alter the antiquated therapeutics methods of the hospital. These craftsmen often helped me achieve small physical improvements to the wards under my responsibility. I managed to have a short flight of stairs replaced by a ramp. This allowed patients, who had been stuck in the dormitory for years to eat in the dining room, and enjoy the television in the sitting room. It also made it possible for the nurses to push wheelchairs up the ramp, instead of having to carry paralysed patients. The lives of the patients were a little more comfortable, and the task of the hard pressed staff easier. The Matron screamed about the £400 cost, she said. The carpenters told me they had used about £30 worth of wood. The cost of their day's work would be absorbed in their normal monthly salary. The offshoot of this was that all the sisters began to ask their assistant matrons for ramps to be built on their ward. Then the male staff heard about it, and joined the chorus, demanding to be afforded this improvement to their units.

As we worked shifts we were all paired up with a colleague of the same rank. We both had equal duties, and responsibilities towards our allocated wards. This worked well enough on the whole for the old timers. Most of them had been professionally formed by the institution and had worked all their lives within the system. But for a new comer with a few progressive ideas, it could be a very problematic undertaking.

The first six months of my work at St. Dymphna were made agreeable by having the good luck of sharing an office with Valerie. She had trained at St Dymphna, but was not yet blind to the faults of the system. She pointed out obvious pitfalls and was generally very helpful. I also had an opposite number who was prepared to let me have my head, within reasonable limits. If she did not approve of my suggestions she usually contented herself with pointing out that Ms Pincher would "not buy it". I was too new in the post anyway, to be too radical.

After this initial period, I was moved to a different area to replace a colleague who was about to retire. There I shared an office with a tough dyke, whose mate was one of my ward sisters. Ms Duckworth or Ducky as she was called, was the eyes and ears of the Matron. Valerie warned that every word, every sigh was reported to the top office. This often resulted in my decisions being countermanded by the boss, especially if they involved staff welfare. Usually this was done behind my back, and sometimes it took days before I found out. One Friday it was announced that the buses from the local garage would stop running at 9 pm at the weekend. This was to protest the attack of the person on a conductor, which had taken place a week earlier. Several domestic workers did not come on duty, afraid that they would have to walk home. Of the few who came, two pregnant women asked me if they could leave early so as to catch the last bus leaving the garage. I gave them the permission requested. The next day only one of these cleaners came to work. When I asked her what had happened to her friend, she told me that being told by Ms Duckworth that they could not leave half an hour early, they had had to walk all the way home, all four miles. Her friend's husband would not let her come back to work. She informed me that she was working until the birth of her baby, so as not to loose her maternity benefit. She would not return at the end of her leave. So for the want of a little humanity, we had lost two very good workers.

I asked Ducky what was the idea behind this tough decision. Her answer was that it was up to the cleaners to arrange their transport to and from work. It was in no way the responsibility of the hospital. Now, I knew!

My opposite number now was a dreadfully coarse and ignorant woman. Mrs Tappy never spoke to me, she barked. Her nickname round the hospital was Hilda Baker, an old comedian whose chief claim to fame had been a very loud voice, and a constant use of malapropisms. I soon understood that the last thing I should do was to suggest any changes. That is, unless I hankered to be deafened by her shouting. When she retired a few years later, the traditional hat was passed around. I said I would only contribute if they bought her a pair of roller skates to help her get out of the hospital quicker.

Assistant Matrons had the responsibility of checking the body of every patient who died, and note bedsores and bruises. At Worthfield, this was the task of the ward sister. We were also called to the wards every time a patient was aggressive, or just threatened violence. At Worthfield phoning our senior in these instances, would have resulted in an answer implying that we were not able to cope in a crisis. I do not know if the ward sisters felt supported, by having their assistant matrons breathing down their necks all the time. I thought it was rather infantilising.

We all had 9 to 11 wards to supervise. And by an idiosyncratic view of fairness, Ms Pincher had divided the units in a way that made sure we were running all day, from one end of the hospital to the other. The main building was on three floors. The bungalows and Nissen huts totalled approximately the equivalent number of wards on a floor of the original complex. Instead of dividing the responsibilities by floor, she felt that it would be unfair if one assistant matron had all the ground floor wards, and another all the top floor. So I had three wards on the ground floor, three wards outside, two on the top floor, one north and one south, two on the middle floor, one north and one south. We were expected to do two rounds per shift, on top of the pen pushing, and the personnel work that came with the administration of our units.

We had to attend a meeting with the matron at 9 am, by which time we would have finished the first round. We had acquainted ourselves with all the wards reports, and attempted to solve any staffing problems that may have occurred. We had about an hour, after this meeting was over, to snatch a cup of coffee and catch up with the paper work. At 11 am we were all present in the Deputy Matron's office for the staff allocation meeting. This was the time when staffing problems for the next day would be sorted out. On Fridays, whenever student nurses were due to change wards, the meeting could last nearly two hours. Invariably, I came out of this exercise with a blinding headache. The second round had to be done, and the report prepared for the afternoon shift. When I left the hospital at 2pm, I never had the feeling that I had achieved much.

The afternoon shift was a little more relaxed. We usually managed to have a sociable tea break. The matron left the hospital at about 5 o'clock, and a definite loosening up of the atmosphere took place. Although no remarks were ever made to that effect, it was palpable.

I was always very careful not to quarrel with the colleagues on my shift. If I was hoping to make any changes to the way things were run, I always asked first why they were done as they were. I usually got one of the two traditional St. Dymphna's answers 1. It can't be done or 2. If we needed it, we would have done it a long time ago. If it only concerned problems of administration such as a duplication of written reports, I left things as they were. But, if my ideas involved the welfare of the patients in the wards for which I had a responsibility, I would go straight to the craftsman concerned, or the supply officer if it involved serious expenditure. One day, I saw in a ward report that two old women had sustained injury to their buttocks. Mrs Tappy had read this in the morning, but she had apparently done her two rounds, without inquiring as to the cause of the problem. When I went to the ward, I asked the very conscientious Sister, what had happened to the patients. She said. "It is nothing new. The sanitary commodes are so old that the metal seats wear out and crack, leaving sharp edges". Apparently Mrs Tappy had told the Sister on the other shift that the budget did not run to affording new commodes. In all my years at Worthfield I had never seen such antiquated wear. I went straight to the supply officer. Over a cup of tea, he agreed to replace all the commodes on my ward, but begged me not to broadcast it before the deed was done. I asked him to make sure that the name of the ward should be painted on the commodes. I had to discourage my colleagues from removing them to their units. The other staff in the office envied my temerity a little, there were little jokes such as "you better ask Cobin, she gets things done!"

There were few areas, where the assistant matrons as a body dared to defy the dragon in the top office. When it was done, it was always without the knowledge of the lady concerned. But one instruction, which the Matron thought had been written in stone, was almost totally ignored. That was the procedure described by her as the Official Walk. It was referred to by all her assistants as "the chastity walk". We had orders, to scour the extensive grounds every afternoon. We were expected to dig out of the bushes that a couple of patients engaged in sexual activities. The inmates who had ground parole, often formed associations with patients from the opposite side of the hospital. As there was nowhere for them to meet in private, they tried to find what little privacy they could in the grounds. We were already running from one end of the hospital to the other all day. We thought that hunting loving couples was not a priority.

From the spring to the autumn on weekend afternoons, with our pager in our pockets, we did enjoy a walk round the grounds for our pleasure. The Matron did not work at weekends, a more relaxed attitude prevailed in the office. I found it most enjoyable to hear from the old timers about activities which had taken place in their youth, Then the Asylum was a real community. We went to the old garden of rest, and sat on old stone benches. We then we climbed the outside steps of the old brewery. From there, we had a superb view of the Grand Union Canal. When the weather was clement, I enjoyed seeing the pleasure boats with their multicolour hulls. If we met loving couples, we pretended blindness. We never commented on it, even between ourselves. Our attitude was not so much complicity, as collusion. One day, at report time, the Matron referred to a long stay patient who was found to be pregnant. Looking at us all she said "How could this have happened?" No one said a word, but when she asked if we were still doing the Official Walk, in one voice we all answered "Yes, Matron". With a sigh of relief, she passed on to the next item.

Administrative work was not giving me much satisfaction. I was missing the contact with the patients. The school of nursing asked me occasionally to give a talk to the nurses, and so I enjoyed that more. It was not totally satisfying, but it certainly was a distinct improvement on running from one end of the hospital to the other, all day. A side bonus of my little excursions to the school was that the nurses saw a side of me, which they liked. This resulted in a much friendlier welcome on their part, when I came across them in the units. Most of the students stopped looking scared, when they saw me arrive on the ward. Relationships with the junior staff improved further, after I returned from the middle management course. I had to produce a piece of written work, based on research within the hospital. I chose to devise a first line management course for the student nurses in their final year. Matron Pincher had her doubts about giving me permission to communicate with students who were not allocated to my wards. I mentioned to her that the Nursing Review, to which I was an occasional contributor, was interested in publishing the results of the experiment. I was bluffing, as the paper had never accepted work before seeing it, but they took everything I sent them, so I took the risk. They did publish my research. It was subsequently plagiarised by a prestigious London Teaching Hospital with a few adaptations made to fit the different setting. It was published as original work in the rival nursing paper. I found it rather amusing, as that hospital which had not considered me good enough to shortlist me when I had applied for a post there, thought nothing of stealing my work.

Chapter Twenty-Nine

St. Dymphna was in effervescence, due to a projected visit from The Hospital Advisory Service. Teams of experts were investigating long stay residential institutions. The inquiry had been instigated by then Minister of Health, Keith Joseph. It was the result of the publication of the very critical report, "Sans Everything". This came on the heels of the Salmon report, which advised a drastic reform of nursing administration. The senior staff, a large number of the junior employees and students, were interviewed individually by members of the team. Resentment and venom, which my colleagues had bottled up for years towards the Matron, came up in these interviews. I was rather shocked, even disgusted, that these women who had smiled and acquiesced at everything Ms Pincher said, betrayed her in such a way. Most of them had known the woman since adolescence, some of them all their lives. They bore some responsibility, in having allowed her to become so despotic. I could hear my colleagues, discussing what they had said to the team. Old Ducky, who had been the eyes and ears of the Matron, was not slow in destroying her. Mrs Tappy, who would never have acceded to such a post anywhere else, joined in the lynching of her protecting superior. She had known the Matron since her youth, and was her favourite.

I said very little on the personality of Ms Pincher. I did not believe in pushing down the head of a drowning woman. I did talk about the stultified methods of administration of the hospital. It had not all originated with her, but it had not occurred to her to initiate changes. The Matron had just reached her 55th year, which was an accepted age of retirement for psychiatric staff. With a minimum of dignity, and even less ceremony, she was told to go. She had some holidays due so she was not even allowed to work her notice. She had started to work at St. Dymphna in her mid-teens, and suddenly she was gone.

I do not think that all the committee members respected the anonymity of the staff. Matron told me that she knew it was the colleagues she had sponsored who had let her down. She felt betrayed by those she had nurtured. It was amazing that she should confide in me, whom she had not even liked, and whose modern methods she had so distrusted.

It was announced to the senior nursing staff that the recommendations of the Salmon report would be implemented in conjunction with the reforms advocated by the investigating team. The discussions taking place within my earshot predicted a rather undignified scramble to the top by the nursing administrators. Promotion had always come easily to me. I did not have the stomach for joining in the bun fight it promised to be. Administration had given me so little joy that I decided to look elsewhere for my salvation. I went to the school of nursing and asked the Principal's opinion of my potential as a nurse tutor. Freddy Craven had seen me teach and had heard the reaction of the students to my classes. He declared himself delighted at the idea that I should do the tutor's course. He advised me about the colleges which were available through the auspices of London University. He informed me about the funding made available by the Regional Hospital Board. He described the strings attached to the generosity; it was after all, the National Health Service.

I applied to the three London colleges. Two asked me to wait a year, and study science at evening classes in the interim. My education was rather lacking in these areas. But I was in a hurry, and accepted the place offered by the Royal College of Nursing. The RCN was not my first choice, however, I was very happy to have at last the chance of a full time study. I was determined to make the most of my time of freedom. Of course, there would be lectures to attend, assignments to fulfil, deadlines to meet. Nothing could dampen my joy, or my sense of freedom. At last, I could concentrate on catering to my own need to learn.

The course was designed primarily to meet the needs of the general tutors. There were many areas of study, which the psychiatric tutors would never use in their future careers. I attended the classes conscientiously. I knew that once the exams were over, I would never give the medical subjects another thought. I gave up the pathology demonstrations, after a very fond student, had swung a very old human foot in my face.

The psychiatry taught was on the level, which would have had a second year psychiatric student nurse yawning. I gave that up too until a few weeks before the exams. A friend informed me that the professor would do the viva in the university finals.

The most relevant part of the course and the most enjoyable were the lectures on Education and Educational Psychology. Andrew Davis, the professor of Adult Education, who taught us, was really inspired. On his own, he made the course worthwhile. He accompanied us for the whole two years. We were really privileged to be taught by him. The psychiatric students particularly appreciated him. The lack of pomposity which some of the medical professors exhibited was refreshing. His insightful view of the work of the nurses, and his humanity, gave us all so much.

The group was very competitive. After each assignment, there was a fevered discussion of the grades. The first test had been a biology essay in which I had done rather well. This was the only science in which I felt at ease. The only other French student in the class sulked for several days because I had better notes than she had. After that I never told my results to anyone, not even to my friends. One of them, Patsy, did not share this information with anyone either. So we understood each other's discretion in the matter. It was generally assumed that my reluctance to disclose my results with the other students was because I was doing badly. But I was holding my own pretty well, apart from the physics and the chemistry, which remained closed books to me. I asked the help of an Ulster girl, who seemed to understand what was going on. But she told me she "was all at sea". In the test, she managed 95% answers correctly compared to my 17%. Only one other student scored less than I. She had also failed to get help from our Irish colleague. On the day of the science exams, a desperate person's bad day was my salvation. I was travelling on the Underground on my way to college, when the train stopped, as we got closer to White City station. We were too far from the platform to get out, so we waited, and waited. After about 40 minutes a white faced London Transport employee informed us that due to an "incident", the train would not be leaving for another half an hour. Most of the passengers knew the "incident" referred to the tragic death of a human being. Calling it an "incident" was London Transport's way of coping. The grumbling, which had taken place in our carriage stopped. For the next 30 minutes we were all very quiet.

I arrived at the college, a few minutes before the end of the exams. The Professor of Chemistry, who was invigilating saw my face in the door peephole, and came out. On hearing my explanation, he was very concerned about me. He gave me the exam questions to do quietly at home, in my own good time. I understood his message. I did not look up the answers. But I worked my way through the test rather leisurely. My marks were only a few points higher than in the previous test, but I passed the science exams on aggregate.

During the study leave which preceded the university exams, a freelance journalist asked me to help her, as she had double booked herself. To fulfil the assignment, I went to Syon Park. I had to report on the launch of a book on gardening for the handicapped. My brief was to write a review of the work for a charity periodical. It was a beautiful spring day, which made it possible for the event to take place in the open air. A name badge on my chest, a notebook in one hand and a glass of wine in the other, I was thoroughly enjoying the experience. An unknown woman approached me. She came so close that I thought she was about to kiss the identification tag pinned on my jacket. I stepped back instinctively, as she introduced herself. She was a journalist working for a nursing periodical. This was the rival of the paper, which published my freelance work, as confirmed by the badge on her chest. Without preamble, she asked me why I never sent articles to her paper. I replied, "Because your rival publishes everything I send them. Your paper refused my very first piece, the other took it, so why change?" She told me that meeting me was really providential, as her journal was hoping to run a number of articles on Nursing in the Common Market. There were already a number of contributors lined up for the project, but most of them had little or no experience. The editor had been looking for a more seasoned writer to launch the series. I was flattered by the compliment, but answered that I would have to think about it before accepting the assignment. I was after all about to have my final exams. I was under some pressure. But I knew at once that I would do it. The paper had no idea that I knew France so very little. I thought it wise to keep quiet about this. On the other hand, I decided that to do justice to the paper, I would only visit hospitals in the region I knew well. This meant going to Avranches, and the surrounding area. I was feeling rather jaded from swotting all the medical matters. It was a constant effort due to my lack of interest in general medicine. I thought that at this late stage a few days of break might actually refresh me.

Chapter Thirty

The hotel door was closed. On it was pinned a notice saying, "FERME POUR CAUSE DE RETRAITE". For a moment I stood there, my eyes fixed on these five words. Since I had agreed to do this assignment, the thought that I would be staying at this little Inn had kept my anxiety under control. When I was a child, the owner Mme. Pincon had always been kind to me. Standing on the narrow pavement, I had to move constantly to allow access to passers-by. I felt as bewildered and lost as a desert explorer deprived of a compass.

I rang the doorbell, and Madame Pinson opened a side door. She confirmed, somewhat apologetically, that the hotel had closed that very day. She directed me to a small Inn nearby. The Hotel du Moyen Age, could have been standing there since the historical period which gave it its name. Its facilities were outmoded, and dingy, clean, but shabby, as only French hotels can be. But such was my state of paralysis that it did not occur to me to go elsewhere. It was as though I had taken Madame Pinson's suggestion as an order.

It was only mid-morning but on accepting the room offered, I was suddenly overtaken by an urgent need to sleep. I kicked off my shoes, threw my coat on the only chair in the room, and got into the bed fully clothed.

When I woke up two hours later, I was less tired. I was still unable to shake off the feeling of unreality, which had overtaken me when I had found myself locked out of Madame Pinson's Inn.

I told myself it was fatigue. I had not slept well on the overnight ferry to Cherbourg. The coach trip to Avranches had seemed endless. This dingy hotel was really too downbeat to stimulate anyone.

As the hotel did not have a restaurant, I went in search of food, though, my faith in the therapeutic effects of a good meal were being undiminished. When the food arrived, I found that I could not eat it. There was a knot in my throat, which made swallowing impossible. I played with the food for a while under the curious eyes of the waitress. I ordered coffee, then left.

Back at the hotel, I decided that I was probably getting the flu. As I did not have any commitment until the following morning, I returned to bed. I emerged in the evening, and tried again to find food. I changed restaurant as I did not want to face the intrusive look of the waitress. I ordered wine, and after half a glass I was able to swallow a little food. I finished the wine, and feeling quite drunk I staggered back to the hotel.

I slept fitfully for a few hours, and at 3 am woke up feeling very cold. There did not seem to be any heating in the room, so I wore underwear under my bedclothes and went back to sleep. I had a nightmare that I was being pursued in the streets by German soldiers, while the pavements were lined with local people who were sniggering. When I had calmed down, I told myself that the bad dream had probably been the result of the oncoming flu, and too much wine. I wondered how I was going to cope with work in the morning, and tried in vain to go back to sleep.

The next day the temperature, which had been so mild, fell to freezing level. I set off to the hospital to do my first interview, wearing a pale turquoise spring outfit, and high heel shoes. Sleet began to fall, and I felt very unsteady on the slippery pavement going down hill.

When I arrived at the hospital, I immediately recognised the once familiar portal. It was no longer guarded by a grey clad nun, but by a uniformed porter. I was directed to the office of a certain Ms J.M Burin. On the letter granting me the interview, I had recognised the surname. It was the same as the one, which belonged to my cousin

Marianne's childhood friend. However, I had been unable to decipher the initials on the signature. Burin was quite a common name locally, so I was unsure of the identity of the person I was going to meet.

Jeanne Marie Burin was flattered that an English nursing review had chosen her provincial hospital as the subject of an article. She was welcoming and friendly, as she had never been when I was the poor child from the orphanage. In our childhood, Jeanne Marie and my cousin Marianne played together, while I was left alone shut up in another room. I was brought out for meals, and returned to my solitude, until it was time for me to go back to my prison. My poor aunt was so ashamed to be seen with me, that she walked fast ahead, so as not to look, as if we were together,

Ms Burin showed me the newly refurbished casualty department. It was equipped with modern machinery, that none of her staff had yet learned to use. She implied that the equipment had just arrived, but the layer of dust covering it belied her statement. Some time later the head nurse offered to show me a newly upgraded surgical ward. I found myself in the ward, where my mother had spent a month. During this part of the visit, in spite of the increased flu symptoms, I went on doing my job, asking questions in French, and taking down the replies in English. When we left this area, Ms Burin suggested that we should perhaps visit a medical ward, which had also been modernised. But when she mentioned the name St. Adele, I recognised it as the ward where at the age of nine I had last seen my mother. I had already put my foot on the first rung of the stairs, but it would not go any further. I had to say that I thought I had seen enough. I thanked her excessively for her help and time, to cover up my terror, and flew from the hospital.

I knew I would not be able to eat lunch. I returned to the hotel, and slept until it was time to get ready for the afternoon's appointment. This was the private clinic, where the nuns from the orphanage took me regularly for X-rays. I went there often, after I had been ill with a lung disease at the age of ten. The geographical proximity of the clinic to our convent made it a more convenient location than the state hospital, which was some kilometres away. The only bad memory I had of the place was not associated with the X-rays department. I remembered the ophthalmologist, who once lost his temper with me. He slapped my face when I could not decide whether I saw better or worse when he was testing my sight. This incident stayed with me all my life. Like most people, I dread visits to the dentist. But the prospect of the most extensive dental treatment has never traumatised me as much as the need to change my spectacles.

The visit went well. I was lucky enough to be able to interview friendly floor nurses. Not only had they a very positive attitude to their work, but they enthused at the prospect of moving to the newly built clinic. They made me some dreadful tasting tea, the awful flavour of it being more than made up by the jolly atmosphere. When I left them I was relaxed enough to undertake a stroll around the town. It was very cold, so I decided to cover up the spring outfit I was wearing with the black maxi coat. I had taken it to use as a blanket on the night ferry. But as soon as I was in the street, I noticed that people were looking at me. I wondered if they had identified me as the daughter of this woman, who had caused such a scandal during the war. I had a violent bout of terror, fearing I may be attacked. I went back to the hotel. I stopped in the empty bar, for a stiff drink to calm my nerves, before taking refuge in my room. After a little while the idea came to me, that on my previous walks through the town no one had taken the slightest notice of me. On both my visits to the hospital and the clinic, I had not attracted attention. The only thing different this time was my appearance. I suddenly realised that in the time I had been in Avranches, I had not seen a single woman wearing ankle length clothes, so I must have looked strange to these provincial people. I tested my hypothesis by going out in the freezing cold wearing more conventional clothes. No one looked at me. In an instant my attack of paranoia was gone.

After a couple of stiff aperitifs, I was able to eat a small meal. That night the German soldiers were still pursuing me through the town. But the pavements were deserted, and no one sniggered at me. The following morning, I was able to eat a good breakfast. By the time I boarded the train to my next assignment, I felt much better and told myself I had beaten the flu.

When I arrived at the psychiatric hospital, which was to be my next port of call, I had almost recovered. The weather was still cold but I no longer shivered. I still felt rather fragile, as if I just had a severe illness. I was informed that the patients in the convalescent ward had cooked lunch for me. I felt a little apprehensive. It would be just too awful if I were unable to eat it. But I enjoyed the meal and even felt comforted by it.

I had cause to be pleased. The interview with the staff had gone very well. I was on familiar grounds, and so I was totally at ease. For their part, the nurses expressed their relief at having been able to speak to someone who knew what their work entailed; an interviewer who did not looked down on psychiatric patients and staff, but was part of the "family", as a nurse touchingly put it.

After lunch a doctor joined us for coffee. He seemed curious to know if I had been brought up in the area. To my positive answer, he suddenly became rather quiet. I had hoped that I would be shown some male wards. The letter offering me the interview, had said I was welcome to go anywhere in the hospital. But nothing was said about it. I thought it more diplomatic not to remind them of their offer. They had already been so generous with their time and hospitality. I remembered that in England the male wards, although spotlessly clean tended to be rather drab. They appeared very bare and institutional despite their comfort. I thought the male wards in the French hospital would probably be even more dreary. Perhaps this would explain the reluctance of the staff to show them to me.

Nearly two years later, I discovered the psychiatrist's reason for not offering to show me the male side of the institution. The reason was nearer to home. Papa Cobin was a patient in the hospital. My stepmother had him committed because his alcoholism had caused him to behave erratically. He had endangered the life of their three children, by setting fire to the family home.

As I left Normandy for the Breton capital, I felt a further improvement in my health. I even had a sense of general well being. I did wonder about this strange virus, which had cured itself so miraculously. By the time I arrived to Rennes, I had quite forgotten I had been so unwell.

Chapter Thirty-One

Janine was waiting for me. We had not seen each other for many years. But how could I have forgotten this thick head of wheat blond hair, and the stubborn face underneath it. It was instant recognition and immediate complicity.

At thirty-nine, Janine had recently been widowed for the second time. When she was twenty-two, she had lost her first husband. She had found herself alone with a one-year-old baby. Now, she had two more children to bring up on her own. She did not seem to have let these disasters daunt her spirit. She took it all as being part of her destiny. Disasters had to be surmounted, and not allowed to crush you. Her two husbands had died while being in the armed services. Army pensions, and her salary as accounting clerk at the Ministry of Social Security, meant that at least she was financially secure.

For the next few days, work kept us both very busy. When the weekend came, I witnessed the extent of Janine's capacity for enjoyment. On Saturday evening, we worked our way through a typical Breton gastronomic menu. On Sunday morning after a breakfast of coffee and croissants, she announced that her liver was rather in need of a clear out. Only oysters would do it. So she drove all the way to Cancale. By eleven o'clock, we were sitting on the terrace of a seaside restaurant, sampling oysters and sipping white wine. Then, started the search for the perfect place for lunch. For nearly two hours, we looked at restaurants and their menus. Janine dismissed them all for reasons I could not fathom. When at last she found the perfect place, we sat under a "tonnelle" and enjoyed another superb meal.

The next day on the ferry to Southampton, I had to abandon any attempts at working on the notes of the interviews. As soon as I started to read them, I began to feel ill again. I told myself I was tired. The work had been quite demanding. Five long interviews in three days. Added to this was, the high living I had enjoyed with Janine. I would have fallen asleep, if the seats behinds me had not been occupied by two chattering French women. Judging by the content of their discussion, I was kept awake by some staff of London French Embassy.

From Cherbourg to the English port, they did not stop once from gossiping maliciously about their colleagues. They were particularly nasty about the personnel of the consulate. For five full hours, the character assassinations went on relentlessly. There was a break of a few minutes, just before we reached the port. The boat was rather full with Easter holidaymakers returning home. So I had not dared leave my seat and look for somewhere quieter. In retrospect, I wished I had had the wit to switch on my press tape recorder. The episode confirmed me in the poor opinion I already had of diplomatic personnel. At the age of seventeen, I had been unceremoniously thrown out of the French Consulate in Lausanne. That was my reward for having the impudence to go there for advice.

As we got up to leave the ferry, my eyes met those of the English woman who had sat next to me during the crossing. I smiled apologetically, forgetting that the lady did not realise I was French. She said to me, "these young women deserve a medal for staying power. I have never heard the likes of it." I replied, "or hanging". My neighbour inquired, "why hanging?" I joked, "If character assassination was punishable by death, these young women would be condemned for the murder of the whole French diplomatic staff in London". The lady broke into a broad smile. "Oh! Well" she said, "Let us hope their turn will come". On these words we parted.

On my return to London, the nursing paper allowed me time to revise for my Sister's Tutor's final exams. The notes of my interviews were put aside. But the psychological effects of my visit to France, could not be so easily forgotten. In the middle of a study session, I would have a renewed attack of the flu symptoms, which had plagued my visit to Avranches. I had always coped well with exams. Usually, I kept my worry under manageable control by working until the last minute. However, this time I went to see my GP complaining of severe exams nerves. Being sympathetic, he gave me some valium. I took little bites of the tablets, when anxiety threatened to drown me. I had finally given its true name to the malaise, which was affecting me. I realised that the time bomb I had been sitting on for so long, risked exploding. This came at a very inopportune moment. I was about to have my final exams. I had waited until my mid-thirties to benefit from the privilege of a university course. I was not easily contemplating the prospect of wrecking it at the last minute. The next objective of my long-term plans would go for a "Burton", if I failed to pass this hurdle successfully. So I swallowed crumbs of valium, and kept going.

Success in the exams brought with it the prospect of returning to work in the hospital, which had sponsored my studies. I was not unduly worried, as I was looking forward to teaching. I was going to work regular hours, as this was important to my long-term hopes. I was also looking forward to working under the supervision of the Principal Tutor.

I arranged a meeting with my new boss to discuss the date of my return to work. I had scarcely time to sit down, when he informed me that he would be retiring before I took up my post. The tutor I was replacing had already gone, and the Senior Tutor would overlap with me by a few days. His replacement had taken up her post a week previously. Indeed the only members of the teaching Staff who were not retiring were the clinical teachers. They were in possession of a certificate, enabling them to teach practical nursing skills. A six-month course enabled them to acquire this qualification. I would not be able to get much guidance or support from them, beyond help with the planning of practical teaching classes.

I let the principal know that I was very angry. I felt he had betrayed me. He got out of his predicament by saying that my contract specified that I was returning to work at St. Dymphna's school of nursing. My commitment was to the hospital, and not to a specifically named individual superior. He was not even legally correct. I read the documentation carefully on my return home. It confirmed that I was committed to teach in a school of nursing, within the region, which had sponsored me. I was not tied to any specific institution within it. Nothing could diminish the bitter feeling that I had been the victim of trickery.

The nursing paper was pressurising me to deliver the articles, as they were to kick off the series. Whenever I settled down to work on them, the symptoms induced by my anxiety returned. To give myself breathing space, I decided to write the articles backwards. I thus began by tidying up the interviews I had done in Rennes. I followed this by working on the meetings in the psychiatric hospital in Pontorson. At last, and with mounting difficulty, I revised my interviews in the private clinic in Avranches. I finished with my traumatic visit to the hospital.

I sent the work in the correct order to the editor of the paper. The proofs arrived, together with a rather complimentary letter from the editor. But they had been sent to me in the reverse order. On discovering this, I nearly keeled over. I felt that I had been found out. I was just about to go for a walk with a neighbour but I had to cancel.

I arrived at the school of nursing to find it in a state of unrest. The new principal tutor had been met with a wall of hostility. Mr Prisky had been a refugee from Eastern Europe, who had settled in Scotland. The addition of a strong Scottish accent, to a very pronounced foreign one made him difficult to understand. He had an almost total incomprehension of the English system. This added to the lack of cooperation of the teaching staff, created a situation where a collision would be unavoidable.

I was only partly aware of the crisis unfolding under my eyes, burdened that I was by the need to keep my anxiety under control. Knowing the date of publication of the French articles increased my panic.

Joseph Prentice, the retiring senior relieved himself of secret information, which was obviously burdening him. He knew who had denounced to the hospital authorities a clinical teacher, Oliver Sandringham. This young man had been found guilty of indecent behaviour, in a public lavatory. The police constable who had arrested Oliver, apologised to him when he realised Oliver was a member of the nursing profession. The officer knew that it would mean more than a £2 fine for Oliver, if he was found guilty. The verdict would be followed by his appearance in front of the general Nursing Council disciplinary committee. This may lead to the young man losing his job. The constable informed Oliver that having started to fill in the charge sheet he could not stop. He advised him that he would declare the accused man to be a clerk. Unfortunately, the royal connection of Oliver's name attracted the attention of a journalist who was in court. He wrote a few lines about it in a local paper. This snippet was seen by another clinical teacher, Marie Cork. This woman was Oliver's closest friend in the school. She brought the press cutting to the hospital, and presented it to Joseph Prentice. She said that her conscience could not let her remain silent. The Senior Tutor tried to make light of the incident, saying everybody knew Oliver's sexual orientation. So why make a fuss, but Marie insisted that the law had been broken. All State Registered Nurses' criminal convictions had to be reported. Joseph realised that if he did not take the information to the Principal, Marie would do it. He had only a few months left to work at the end of a long nursing career. He did not want to end it on a black note. So he reported Oliver to the principal who took the matter to the top, for the same reasons.

I had known about the incident, as a friendly colleague had warned me when I was still at the college. She was worried about Oliver. She had heard, that he was being hauled in front of the nurses' tribunal. The young man was on a course at the college at the time. My friend asked me to keep an eye on him. I had met him over a lunchtime drink, and tried to be supportive. He had been very depressed. If he lost his licence to practice, he would kill himself. He could never face telling his widowed mother, with whom he lived. In the event, he got away with a warning, and was advised to be more discreet in future. One of the judges said to Oliver. "Go away and be a good boy now!"

But Oliver could not let it rest there. He had to find out who had betrayed him. His suspicions fell on Brendan, his oldest friend in the hospital. These two young men shared the same sexual orientation. They had been close for many years. Brendan was the only person to whom Oliver had confided his problem with the law. But the more Brendan denied having betrayed Oliver's secret, the more the latter tormented him. This was not all Oliver did. He went around the hospital, quizzing all of his friend's associates. As they were both clinical teachers, the ambivalent relationship of the two men, added to the atmosphere of tension in the school.

Joseph Prentice had started the conversation by telling me to be very careful with Marie Cork. He had said, "Marie can be very perfidious, you know". I said I knew that she did not like me very much. I had twice beaten her to the promotion post. Once, was by getting the Assistant Matron's job for which she had been shortlisted. Then by getting a place on the Sister Tutor's course, while she was accepted for the Clinical Teacher certificate.

All the time he talked to me, he never stopped clearing his desk drawers. He filled up bag after bag with a quarter of a century of teaching notes and accumulated information. But the secret he was carrying could not be so easily disposed of. So I was his metaphorical dustpan. The old man felt very guilty, about his inability to stand up to the evil that Marie was. Where was the brave fellow, who had endured several years in Wormwood Scrubs prison during the Second World War as a conscience objector? He was thoroughly ashamed of himself. Oliver had been a protégé of his; he was rather found of the lad. He felt that he was no better than Marie. I said, "Oh! Mr prentice, you are flattering yourself, no one could possibly be as wicked as this woman".

The shock of these revelations blurred the long term effect they were to have on me. In relieving himself, the old man was saddling me with the burden of a secret, which would prove over time almost too unbearable to carry.

I felt that I was in hell. The atmosphere in the school was poisonous. Mr Presky was becoming exceedingly frustrated. He was allowing himself to lose his temper frequently, and very loudly. Almost all the staff were in open rebellion against his authority. There was no effort made to try and understand his position. Even the normally very fair secretary, Janet, was at the end of her tether. The new senior, aided and abetted by the old timers, was plotting to get rid of him.

Marie did not hide her hostility towards me. She had an ally, a middle aged woman, who had recently come back from Overseas where she had worked for years as a missionary. Enid bore all the marks of the professional virgin. The two women, my professional juniors, treated me with open contempt. Marie had been recently to a regional study day. There, she had met staff from Worthfield Hospital. She had come back, with a bag of gossips about my sexual behaviour while I worked there. I did not let that bother me. If my long relationship with Paul, and the suspected fling with Julian O'Flarty, made me the whore she declared me to be; was ever a bad reputation bought so cheaply?

I was more bothered that any attempt I made to speak at staff meetings, was short circuited by the dreadful pair with a deprecatory remark, sniggering or stony silence. Oliver, for fear of upsetting his dear Marie, never supported me in public. If he agreed with me, he may occasionally come to my office after the meeting to discuss my suggestion. But if he did not like my idea, he would storm in and display an anger, which was out of proportion with the matter at hand. One never knew which way he would jump. His quest for his betrayer was making him permanently edgy. I knew better than to criticize Marie to him, even though I knew she was trying to poison his mind against me. I was disgusted whenever I saw her take his arm to go to lunch, or I heard her calling out. "Oli darling!!

The friendliness of my students saved what little sanity I had left. It was so fortunate that my class was such good group of youngsters. They came from the four corners of the globe. Most of them were not academically brilliant, but they were keen to learn. What was also important to me was that they were prepared to give a chance to a newly qualified teacher. They demonstrated their liking of me, and appreciation of what I had to offer them. One day one of the boys said to me, "Ms Cobin, we are all in love with you". A little embarrassed, I still had the wit to take the declaration in the light spirit in which it was made. I replied "What! The girls as well!" We both burst out laughing.

The support of my class was made evident when my articles at last came out. I had kept quiet about it, but the students made sure my pieces were not ignored. The students and pupil nurses had a notice board in the school main corridor. They were allowed to pin on it, anything in the nursing press, which attracted their attention. They could add other information on mental health in the general press, which they had found of interest. It was with some surprise that on arriving at the school one morning I found that the two first articles I had written on Nursing in the Common Market were displayed, together with the professional photograph the journal had insisted I provided,

It said volumes on the general attitude of the teaching staff that Oliver and Brendan only commented on the photo, which they declared to be very good. Not a word was said by anyone about the articles. I would not have expected the staff to stand in the corridor to read them. They all had the journal in their hands weekly. By ignoring the articles, Oliver aligned himself with the rest of the group, so as not to upset dear Marie Brendan was too distraught to even think about it. Oliver's constant accusations were destroying him. The irony of it all was that I too was ignoring the notice board. Whenever I walked down the corridor, I looked the other way. The slightest glimpse in that direction, would cause my anxiety to rise to a level, which would wreck the rest of the day.

The prospect of the last two articles appearing the following week, filled me with terror. In the event, the pieces on Rennes did not add to my anguish and I had an easier week. This would have confirmed to me, if I needed it, that the devil was in Avranches, not in the Breton capital.

When my students had finished their period in the school, I came to work very early one morning, and removed the offending articles from the notice board. Without a second look, I hid them at the bottom of a drawer. For a few hours I was relieved, but the terror came back.

The hospital administration had set up a disciplinary hearing, to deal with the management crisis in the school. Leonie Dribble, the

Senior Tutor, aided and abetted by most of the clinical teachers, and the school secretary had brought the crisis to a head. The dreaded day of my personal interview with the disciplinary committee came, and with it acute panic. I realised that I did not have very much to say about Mr Presky. All I knew was that he was losing his temper frequently, and shouting very loudly in the school corridors. I had rarely been present at the start of his outbursts. I never knew what had provoked them. I so much needed some peace, that I found myself agreeing with whatever leading questions I was asked. I was bemused, by the turn the events had taken. I sensed that there was something wrong with the proceedings. In my fragile state, all I really wanted was for the rowing to stop. Later, much later, I felt guilty about the treatment inflicted on the principal tutor. However, at the time I was too new in post, too fragile and probably too cowardly to stick up for him.

The wretched man was sacked, and knowing it would be useless to appeal against the decision of the committee, he accepted it. He removed his children from school, and took his family back to Scotland.

Chapter Thirty-Two

The Senior Tutor, who should have been made happy by the end of the hostilities, went into a decline. She disappeared for several weeks. She left the school rudderless, there was no senior member of staff left. This middle aged spinster, had started work at St. Dymphna shortly before the rejected principal. She had been largely instrumental, in stirring up the general unrest which led to his dismissal. She was now sending medical certificates, saying she was suffering from nervous exhaustion. I felt that perhaps, like me, she had expected to work under the authority of Mr Craven. She had taken her anger out on the new man.

Janet, the secretary, turned up in my office with a wad of letters awaiting signature. I told her that I was in no position to take such responsibility. "Oh! But you are," she said "In the absence of the principal, the most senior member of the teaching staff is in charge of the school. At this instant, this person is you Ms Cobin". I telephoned the district Nursing Officer who confirmed that until the return of Ms Dribble, or the appointment of a locum principal, I was in charge of the school. She was quite sure that my previous administrative experience would serve me well.

After another unpleasant episode with Oliver, Brendan took a massive overdose of drugs. He had become increasingly depressed by his old friend's suspicion. He was saved in extremis by a friend, who had thought to surprise him with an unannounced visit. When he had recovered, he refused to return to the school. He was appointed to a new post of in the rehabilitation department, where he flourished. I saw him occasionally for a drink, but avoided deeper involvement. He once said to me. "My head is all right, but my heart still hurts. I said as warmly as I dared. "I know Brendan, I know," and left him.

Before the return from sick leave of the Senior Tutor, a temporary Principal was appointed. Mr Trowell had retired from teaching nurses in the RANC. I was dreading the arrival of a man, who had spent his teaching career in the military profession. I need not have worried. Mr Trowell was the perfect antidote to the events of the previous months. He was both intelligent, and a good listener. It took him all of five minutes to have Marie Cork assessed. He gave an ear to everybody, and made up his own mind. Discovering that I was the only other qualified tutor, he soon highlighted that it was impossible to run the school on so few qualified personnel. He demanded the appointment of two more tutors. The process of selection was started. Three months later, two newly qualified tutors arrived. Brendan was replaced by an equally freshly qualified clinical tutor. He was a very friendly Hispanic, whose only fault so far as I was concerned, were his wandering hands.

Mr Trowell considered Leonie Dribble to be supernumerary. Her appearances in the school, where at the best spasmodic. Her nerves became exhausted at the slightest exertion. It was hard to believe, that it was the same woman who had so relentlessly persecuted the retched Mr Presky. I do not think the Principal trusted her judgement totally. The time came to interview the batch of youngsters, who would next start their training. The Principal asked Leonie Dribble if I could do the interviews with her, to give me a chance of acquiring experience. He asked me to sit with her and make sure she would not do anything silly. Which of course, she did. She was my senior after all, and the final decision stayed with her.

We interviewed a young man, whose application form had a faint whiff of a bad smell. I could not quite put my finger on it, but felt that something was not quite right. To placate me, she agreed to ask him if he had a criminal record. He was a very charming youngster, and I could see she was quite seduced. She did ask. "Have you ever had any problem with the police? To which he had replied, looking quite angelic. "Yes, I once beat up a man who was threatening my mother". The senior went. "Ah!!!!" She did not hide her admiration for a boy who was defending his mamma. Against my better judgement, he was taken on for training. A few months later, a student nurse who had become involved with him, complained to me that he was beating her up. Later he was abusive towards a patient. When the charge nurse remonstrated with him, mammy's boy beat him up. He was then summarily sacked. Prior to this, I had bought a small van to practise driving before taking the statutory test. The vehicle was a bad starter, and I decided to get rid of it. I advertised the sale, in the weekly staff newsletter. This young man, having presented himself before me, cash in hand saying he wanted the van, I sold it to him. After he was fired from the hospital, I had a phone call from the Buckinghamshire police. The officer asked me if I was the owner of the vehicle. I said I had sold it to this young man. I wanted to know the reason for the enquiry. When the policeman told me the van had been used as a get away vehicle after a burglary, I laughed. "What is so funny?" wanted to know the officer. I told him my reason for selling the van, and he too laughed. Through a contact I had at CRO, I found out that this young man had 8 previous convictions. He had enjoyed her Majesty's hospitality several times. The only offence, he had not been charged with so far, was murder. I kept this information secret as I had promised, but gave myself ten out of ten for intuition.

Despite the calmer atmosphere in the school, I still suffered from bouts of anxiety. I could cover up quite well in public, except when the attack was so bad, that I could not swallow food. It did happen occasionally, when I was sharing a meal with friends. A few drinks before the food was served helped, but I knew only too well, that therein did not lie the solution. Before going on the tutor's course, I had had a long talk with Dr. Isaac Moran, the consultant psychoanalyst at St Dymphna. I discussed with him, my hope of restarting psychotherapy training when I started working regular hours. I had known Isaac since I first came to St. Dymphna. He was holding sensitivity meetings, with the senior nursing staff regularly. Most of my colleagues, insisted on talking about the problems they had with the laundry or the kitchen. It was well nigh impossible to get them to move from this concrete base. To my horror, they were still on the same spot, when I rejoined them two years later. Dr. Moran, had appreciated having at least one person in the group, who understood what he was trying to do.

On my return to St Dymphna I saw him again. He offered to help me find an analyst when I was ready. The applications for most respected Psychotherapy Trainings were invited for the spring. In view of my previous defection, I thought I should be settled with an analyst, before I applied to an organisation. So I had planned to start looking for an analyst early in the New Year. But I now knew, that the grumblings from the bomb I was sitting on, made it impossible for me to wait any longer. I telephoned Dr. Moran, saying to him. "The New Year will not do, It has to be now". Within minutes he was in my office. He did not pry, he just listened. I told him just enough, to let him understand that I was in trouble. He took a very practical view, asking me if I would be more at ease with a man or a woman. We discussed the theoretical Orientation within which I wanted to work. The gender of the analyst, was of no importance to me. Theoretically I preferred an analyst of the middle group. It had to be someone, I never had the slightest working or social connection with. I knew rather a lot of people in the milieu.

A week later, Dr. Moran returned with two names. In the meantime I had felt rather better, and had almost decided to wait until the New Year. But when he walked into my office, I had not the courage to tell him I had changed my mind. I dismissed the male analyst, as he had recently worked at the annexe connected with Worthfield.

Ms Carter, was totally unknown to me. Dr. Moran said that she was a middle group analyst and consulted in Welbeck St. He spoke well of the lady, and was happy to recommend her to me. Before giving me her phone number and her address, he told me she was going to be away for ten days, and gave me the date of her return.

By the time I arrived at my home, I had totally forgotten that I had been asked to wait ten days to call. Before even taking my coat off, I threw myself on the telephone. I dialled Ms Carter's number. I let it ring for a while, before remembering what Isaac Moran had said. It was at that moment, that I faced the desperate plight in which I was.

The ten days passed, I even waited another couple of days more to phone, just to prove to myself that I could. I liked the voice, it was encouraging. The voice made me want to meet the woman.

My friend Sandy, who was already in training analysis made me promise to check the analyst's orientation. I said she has been recommended by Isaac Moran, and she has rooms in Welbeck Street. Sandy said "Don't be so silly, there are as many drippy Yungians and unyielding Kleinians in Welbeck Street, as in the rest of the Harley Street, area and the whole of Hampstead". I knew that it was the voice which had reassured me, not the address. But I decided to ask the theoretical point anyway. I had to be sure I was not going to find myself in a philosophical maze I would find inimical.

The first thought that came to me when I met Ms Carter was not her theoretical standpoint. It was whether she looked as though she was young enough, and more importantly, strong enough, to last the course. Having successfully passed this hurdle, when invited to sit, I chose the armchair behind the couch, it seemed to be the one offering the most protection. The similarity of the two women's name which I had thought may be a block, ceased to be of importance, the moment I met Ms Carter. But after the years of blunt treatment from Ms Casters, I was still rather afraid of being attacked. I had so often felt emotionally slapped and kicked by the social worker.

I still worried about being assaulted. But I was not that day, and I was never going to be chastised. Nevertheless it took a year, and a subtle push from the Analyst, for me to get out of the armchair, and make the few steps to the couch.

Mr Trowell asked me to go to a series of meetings on Nurses Education, and to be accompanied by a clinical teacher. That is how Oliver and I became close friends. He spoke a great deal to me, and I spoke a little to him. After a few trips, he remarked how well we were getting on. I agreed with him, that away from the school, everything seemed easier. He proposed, that we should consider getting married. He wanted us to look at houses. Whenever we saw a house for sale that looked to his taste, he wanted to take the details. I told him from the moment he uttered the first murmur on the subject, that I could not marry him. He kept saying. "But you like me, and you are alone, so why not? I asked him, if he would consider giving up his long term lover Jake? No, he would not, what a silly idea. But he had lived with a girl some years before and managed very well having the odd homosexual fling on the side. I told him that since my last misadventure in Worthfield, I had decided to remain celibate. He still would not take no for an answer.

So in the end I had to tell him, that I was still passionately in love with the Professor of Education who had taught me at the College. He wanted to know details. There was not much to say. He knew the man, who had also taught him. For nearly two years, I had attended his classes one day a week. I was always looking forward to seeing him arrive. But not thinking anything more, than he was an inspiring teacher. During the revision period, shortly before the end of the course, he substituted a rather erotic word on the blackboard instead of the one he intended to write, erasing it at once.

The whole class was laughing. I had not even had the time to see the offending word. Shortly after that, and that time I was listening, he stopped in the middle of a lecture to say. "I could never leave my children". Students were asking what is the matter with Andrew? Somebody said, it is the end of the year, he must be tired, and he was not concentrating.

When the class was over, the only nun on the course approached me. She asked, "What is going on between you and Andrew Davis?" I assured her that nothing was going on between myself and the professor, She said "You may fool others, you do not fool me. I can just about see the sparkles flying across the classroom". The university exams were looming. The time bomb on which I was sitting since my trip to France was making noises. The last thing I needed, was having to deal with the explosion, which took place in my whole being at that instant. What I was feeling, was akin to the turmoil which had shaken me, when I had kissed Louis outside the Swiss cemetery, nearly twenty years before.

I told my friend Sandy what was happening to me, and the shock I just had. Her answer was that no one else was surprised. All my friends, had had two years of hearing about this wonderful person who made the course worthwhile. I quizzed everyone I knew well, and they all repeated my exact phrase. "Andrew Davis, is the only decent thing we have on the course". The problem now was that he was so decent, that he had no intention of doing anything about his feelings for me. I knew it and painful as it was, I accepted it. I also knew that I would never compromise and make do with less. But I never talked about it. I only told Oliver of my passion for Andrew Davis, to let him know that I was not emotionally available. He took it very badly, having nurtured a fantasy of wedlock. One day he was so angry, that he said to me. "This will end with me putting a knife in your back, or hanging myself or both". I remained friendly, and eventually he calmed down. On Christmas morning, he turned up at my house carrying an exquisite painted glass dish. With his arm extended he was holding the parcel in the most delicate manner, as if he was scared to hurt it. I knew then, that we were all right.

When the two new tutors came to the school, I encouraged Oliver to accept their invitation to go clubbing with them. They were jolly girls, younger than both of us, who were keen to explore London's night life. I was not interested in discos and nightclubs, but was pleased to see him having some distraction from his Obsessive pursuit of his betrayer.

His mother, in a bid to control him, had refused to have a telephone in the house. This meant that Oliver was unable to accept spontaneous invitations. He knew that on the dot of six o'clock, his cooked meal would be on the table. Encouraged by the young tutors he accepted to go out one evening, without warning his mother. When he came home in the middle of the night, he was unable to get into the house. His mother had bolted the door, making it impossible for him to go to his bed. This rather tall man, had to spend the night in his Mini.

I had met his mother very briefly, one day on the way back from a study afternoon. Subsequently, she told Oliver that she kept having a nightmare. In it she saw me in Woolworth with a neighbour. We were both dressed as witches, and very frightening. He knew my neighbour well, as she also worked at the hospital, and he must have mentioned this to his mother.

Oliver became rather depressed. He wanted to be free of his mother, but he felt unable to liberate himself. The search for his betrayer was taking a lot of his energy, as he was endlessly pursuing his enquiries. With a view to distract him, and because I loved Italy, I agreed to join him on a camping holiday near Venice.

Plans were at an advanced stage, when one day he turned up at the school saying we could not go. His mother claimed that her washing machine was not working well. She must have a new one. And it had to be now. I tried to make light of it saying "You see how marriage would never have worked, I have the fourth place in your life: after your mother, after Jake and now after the washing machine!" His reply had been. "You really, are too demanding!" One Friday afternoon I was checking the time-table for the following Monday morning. I noticed that I was double booked for one hour. I decided to ask Oliver if he could help me. Everyone except Marie had classes the whole morning.

As I could not ask her. I left a message in his office, asking him to contact me when he returned from the wards. As soon as he walked in the room, I knew something was very wrong, but knew better than to ask what it was. I explained my time table difficulty to Oliver. He said it should not be a problem, if Marie would do a class for him. He suddenly stared at me and said, "Marie, can be very perfidious, you know". The very same words that Joseph Prentice had employed when talking about the woman. I knew that he had found out who his betrayer was. How he did it, I did not know, and would never discover. He was obviously distraught. His beloved Marie! The last person he would have suspected. The blow must have been terrible.

Not saying a word about Marie, but referring to the depression which had affected him recently, I suggested he saw someone who would help him. His reply, was that no one could do anything for him now. Early in the week, I had invited him for Sunday lunch, and I reminded him of it. I then asked" And what are you going to do tomorrow?" He replied. "I do not know...tomorrow, I will probably crawl into a black hole". I knew then that all was lost. He got up abruptly, and walked out of my office. This was the last I saw of him.

Saturday I was very anxious. But there was no phone at Oliver's home. I did not not know his precise address, I could do nothing. On Sunday, I set about preparing his favourite roast, and all the trimmings so beloved of the English. I waited in vain all day.

On Monday morning, I left for work very early. Arriving at the hospital, I made straight for the car park. His Mini was not there. Oliver's idea of Punctuality, was to be the first one to arrive anywhere. I never knew him to be late. At the school, there was no message from him.

I panicked, but no one else was concerned. His car had probably broken down. Perhaps he had overslept. When he was ill, his mother went to the nearest phone box in the course of the morning to phone the school. Between each lesson, I rushed to the Secretaries' office, and asked them for news. At eleven o'clock his mother telephoned, to ask if Oliver was there. She said, she had not seen him since Saturday afternoon, when she left the house to go shopping. He had kissed her, as she was leaving, saying "Good bye mother".

Marie speculated that perhaps he had gone to a monastery. He occasionally went there on retreat. The hypotheses was eventually dismissed. This was when his mother telephoned in the afternoon. She said she had found his car, round the corner, a few yards from the house. She had called the police. The officers had a look round the house, and finding nothing suspicious they had left. In the evening I had an appointment with Ms Carter. At last, I had the chance to have my anxiety understood. I was convinced that Oliver had died. The presence of his car, made a fugue rather unlikely. His very demanding mother, swallowed a large chunk of his income. He could not afford to take taxis. I was speculating the better and the worst possibilities. It was such a relief, to express my anguish. It was the thought of "the black hole", which I could not get out of my head. On the Tuesday, there seemed to be a reluctance in the school to talk about Oliver. The teaching staff, pretended that all was well. The secretaries shook their heads, when I went in their office. There were no words left for the moment. On Wednesday morning Oliver's mother telephoned the school. She had called the police again. She had told them about the trap door, which led to the loft. The officers climbed under the roof and found Oliver. He was dead, a number of empty pill boxes and a bottle of water were nearby. I was shattered, and took refuge in my office, refusing to take part in the general gossip. The most awful thing for me was having to witness everybody sympathising with poor Marie, who had lost her best friend. I found it almost unbearable to keep my mouth shut, but I did. Towards the end of the afternoon, I saw this woman and her acolyte dismantling Oliver's office. They were sharing out his belongings between them. These two women, had been until now working in the same room. Enid installed herself in Oliver's office, that very day. When the two women disappeared to have their tea break, I walked into the office and took two rulers as keepsakes. I said out loud. "Sorry Oliver, but it is now or not at all". The inquest was speedily dispatched. Oliver was "high church", and the vicar took some persuading to do the funeral mass. No one in the school was talking about going to the service, there was no esprit de corps. The school was closed for the day. The members of staff who wanted to attend the obsequies, went on their own. I was far too distraught to make my own way there. No one in the school offered me a lift. It was my students who looked after me all day. A Thai student took me to the Church, she stayed with me until she had to go on duty. She left me in the care of an English student. This young man made sure I had some refreshment. He drove me to Chiswick House, saying he always found the park very soothing, when he was distressed. I could not absorb the shock, of seeing Oliver's mother walking in the church arm-in-arm with Marie Cork. I thought, "The two assassins". The Vicar had been Unkindly callous about Oliver. His first words were. "We can not pretend that it is an ordinary funeral. This young man had committed the almost unforgivable sin of despair. We pray that god in his mercy will, forgive him". After hearing this sermon I could hardly stand up. It was all too much. I could hear Andrea, one of the young tutors with whom Oliver had so enjoyed going clubbing. She was sobbing loudly behind me, but she too had chosen to go to the service on her own. There was no comfort to give, and none to receive there, at this moment. Communication would come later, much later. Shortly after Oliver's burial, I saw Brendan on the steps of the National Westminster Bank. I ran across the road, narrowly avoiding cars. I had to speak to him. We said a few words about the funeral mass, which he too had found upsetting. Then I blurted out. "The day before he died, Oliver knew you had not betrayed him". He asked "Who then? Was it Marie Cork?". I said. "yes, I always knew, I could not say anything. I had been told under the seal of secrecy by Joseph Prentice. But what made you suspect her?" He replied "The press cutting, she is the only one in the school, who buys this paper".

I had been in analysis about six months and was feeling considerably better. On entering the consulting room, I was still giving Ms Carter a visual medical examination. I panicked, If she so much as sneezed during a session. When I left the consulting room, I sometimes had trouble remembering her appearance, by the time I arrived at the end of Welbeck Street. But I never had the need to drown her in apologetic letters, as I did to Ms Casters. I felt safe and understood, and for the first time ever, I talked, letting the bomb slowly, defuse itself. When the time came to apply for psychotherapy training, I told her that perhaps I should give up the whole idea, in view of what I had recently been through. After a short silence she said. "What do you think the other applicants are like?" I knew I had to mention on my application form that I had followed the academic program of another course for some time, and then defected. I feared it may go against me. In the event, my honesty saved me. One of the two analysts by whom I was interviewed, had been previously on the training committee of that first organisation. I was accepted for the course, having agreed to sign an undertaking that I would not stop my analysis before the end of the training. I seemed to have been the only student in my year, who was asked for such a promise. Perhaps I was not totally trusted yet, it would be up to me to prove that I could be. I had embarked on a long journey, which would take me well beyond the end of the course. I was undergoing a very creative analysis, having secured two respected analysts as supervisors to oversee my work during my training. I had the best of everything. At last!

Epilogue

I was on my way to the House of Commons, to attend a meeting of the whole party Parliamentary Mental Health Group. I had the honour, of being a regular Guest of the group for some years. Sitting in the back of the black cab, my mind wandered to the previous evening. I was taking part in a policy meeting of the psychotherapy organisation, where I was tutoring a group of students. My eyes wandered round the room. I recognised Mrs Cohen, the erstwhile colleague, and close friend of my former social worker, Ms Casters. She felt me looking at her. A look of recognition, and surprise came to her face. After the work was over, the group was enjoying a pleasant social moment over a glass of wine. Mrs Cohen approached me. She expressed her astonishment, at what she called my professional ascension. Then she added rather sarcastically "Well! You are not the poor little orphan now! Are you?" Upon these words she walked away from me. I had never had a private conversation with this woman before. At Worthfield, I had avoided socialising with friends of Ms Casters. I her owed that much. But the latter's indiscretion, which in the past would have well nigh destroyed me, now paled into insignificance beside this woman's envy. However, this was Mrs Cohen's problem, not mine. I had always thought that to compare one's own achievements with others was not only futile, it was so destructive. We none of us begin at the same starting block. Circumstances had made me start way behind many of my contemporaries. I never attempted to arrive where they did, and when they did. There were some important milestones in life, which I would

never have the satisfaction of negotiating. But I had faced my own
hurdles, and had never given up the struggle to surmount them. I
walked into the Palace of Westminster, clutching my invitation and
passing the tourists queuing up to get in. I felt a surge of pride in
myself, and my achievements. There was in my life much satisfaction,
and so much quiet happiness.

THE END

For sales, editorial information, subsidiary rights information
or a catalog, please write or phone or e-mail
iBooks
Manhanset House
Shelter Island Hts., NY 11965, US
Sales: 1-800-68-BRICK
Tel: 212-427-7139
www.ibooksinc.com
bricktower@aol.com

For sales in the UK and Europe please contact our distributor,
Gazelle Book Services
Falcon House, Queens Square
Lancaster, LA1 1RN, UK
Tel: (01524) 68765 Fax: (01524) 63232
www.gazellebookservices.co.uk
email: melanie@gazellebooks.co.uk